Getting Real About Enlightenment

To angels and dragons, pirates and poets,

and all the other consciousness explorers

of this world, who dare to plunge into the

Beyond, again and again...

Getting Real About Enlightenment

A modern companion to your journey of sovereign spirituality

KIM SEPPÄLÄ

Genre: Metaphysics, spirituality, personal growth

Erik Istrup Publishing
Jyllandsgade 16 stth., 9610 Nørager, Denmark
eip@erikistrup.dk
www.erikistrup.dk/publishing

Getting real about Enlightenment is my first 'spiritual' book. It is a self-help book for people facing the challenges that come with self-transformation. It is well structured and leads you ever deeper into the mysteries of enlightenment. The author gives insight into her journey and the message is clear: if you're struggling, you're not alone, but it can be done and the journey is worth it. The interviews with people who have come far on their journey round off this guide. An interesting and well written book. - *Angela Jorzik*

This is the kind of book that you should read when going through awakening towards enlightenment! One of the main points is going from self-improvement to self-acceptance. The author points out that awakening rips you apart, shakes your world – not as a punishment, but to let you release what keeps you from being less than you are. It is a practical book, telling you what to expect on your journey. It is reassuring to know that being tired, depressed or feeling empty without passion is "normal" when going through awakening. Each person's path to enlightenment is unique; we can't compare, but we can share our experiences and inspire each other. I highly recommend this book! - *Anne Maribo Andersen*

A truly useful book for the serious pioneer on the path to realization without all the New Age distractions. Here you get insights, guiding as well as in-depth interviews with eight awakened humans. - *Erik Istrup, author & publisher*

Dear Reader

Please note that this book is written for the sovereign human who takes responsibility for his or her life and creations. The author offers the insights contained in this book as spiritual perspectives, and neither author nor publisher assume any responsibility for how this information is used. Please consult a physician or mental health practitioner if you are uncertain about how certain techniques may affect your wellbeing.

Contents

Darkness fell

and the darkness made me stumble

and the stumbling made me open my eyes

and my open eyes saw the light

and the light fell upon my darkness.

Introduction

Dear reader, are you ready to awaken to the conscious experience of life, to the blossoming realization of all that you are? It is easier to keep spirituality as a concept or discipline or devotion – a habit that is badly out-dated. It is seductive to perceive spirituality as something intangible and mysterious, something sacred yet unattainable… But have you ever dared to wonder what it would feel like to be aware of Spirit within you while driving a car or washing the dishes or looking another person in the eyes?

There are many reasons for the popular tradition of casting spirituality out of the more prosaic aspects of life and why spirituality was "trademarked" by the selected few, the priests, the Brahmins and hermits, for most of history. Yet there are other reasons – worth exploring – for breaking this tradition that is so suitable to the past but so misplaced in this era. I, for one, firmly believe that *it is time to bring our spirituality down to Earth*. And by 'spirituality' I mean consciousness. If you, also, are ready (or even curious about what it's like) to embody and express divinity through your human self, then this book is for you.

We are living in chaotic, revolutionary and exciting times – politically, economically, socially, technologically and spiritually speaking. The world is changing at a faster pace and on a larger scale than ever experienced on this planet. This means we have more potentials in life than ever before and more opportunities for expansion; however, it also means more pressure than ever to take responsibility for our choices and consciously design our lives and even our beliefs.

We are living at the threshold of a huge technological breakthrough; we are on the brink of a new world that we cannot even imagine yet. We cannot be certain whether this new world will be more violent or safer than our current reality, whether it will bring countries and cultures closer together or further apart. All we can know for certain is that there will be a lot of change – change that will act as a catalyst for questioning everything. Humanity will come to face questions such as: What remains constant at a time when everything around us seems to be moving? What is true in a world where suddenly everything is unpredictable? What can we hold onto, when old structures and systems are falling apart? How can we find inner peace in a world that worships technology and intelligence? How will the human mind be affected by the creation of artificial intelligence? What are our freedoms and responsibilities in a world where none of the old rules apply? And what happens to love when the world is distracted by fear?

This is the point where many will turn to spirituality. The once clear line between atheists and the religious becomes very fuzzy in an era where biology and technology are melded together. When the line between a human mind and an artificial mind gets blurred, the question of consciousness becomes critical.

The fact is that spirituality has expanded itself beyond organized religions already some time ago and continues to redefine itself; spirituality, like all other human creations, is going through deconstruction.

New Age - Old News?

You probably are very familiar with the New Age phenomena. New Age spirituality, here defined as an eclectic form of Western esotericism, has its roots in 19th Century theosophical philosophy led by new thought leaders Madame Helena P. Blavatsky, H.S. Olcott and C. Q. Judge in collaboration with El Morya Khan and other masters of the East. As such it is not very new, although the New Age movement gained momentum in the 1960s and 1970s with the influence of Eastern spirituality brought to America by Yogananda's movement. New Age philosophy has also been impacted greatly by the field of psychology in the 20th century: Especially theories of the subconscious self (brought forward by S. Freud), the concepts of the collective consciousness, archetypes, and the shadow self (C. Jung), the emphasis on freedom and existential questions (existential psychologists), awareness as the agent for change (around which most schools of psychology are built on), and the importance of integrating disowned aspects of the self (Gestalt therapy), have contributed to the development of the New Age.

Today the New Age has evolved from a fringe movement to a fairly common philosophy in the West. It is also a considerable industry due to its far-reaching popularity. Although countless sceptics look down upon the New Age, we should not underestimate the spiritual earthquake it has set in motion especially in the West. And yet, despite it growing ever more fashionable, the New Age, as it has been experienced in the past five decades, is transforming into something truly new. This book is concerned with a form of spirituality – or rather a lack of form – that is now emerging on Earth, unlike anything that we have known before.

Sovereign Spirituality

"When there were no churches, no creeds or sects, but when every man was a priest unto himself" *Helena Petrovna Blavatsky,* The Secret Doctrine

The New Age, as we have known it, had a significant purpose: it brought into awareness alternative ways of experiencing spirituality that went beyond the old Western paradigms of either following an institutionalized religion, or on the other extreme opting for atheism or agnosticism and ignoring spirituality altogether. Organized religions have provided individuals with many comforts (such as: community, answers, meaning, hope etc.), but freedom certainly isn't one of them. Atheism, although free of dogma and rules, has served as merely another kind of limiting belief system: the belief in a reality that can be seen and felt only with the physical senses and understood with the thoughts of the mind.

The New Age brought the element of freedom to spirituality and demonstrated to the Western world what had long been acknowledged in the East: Yes, there are other forms of spirituality; you *can* connect to the divine without having to ascribe to the rules of a religion that you don't resonate with. You can live a "spiritual life" that doesn't involve going to church on Sundays or reading the Koran. You can explore metaphysical concepts without being initiated into the secrets of the Kabbalah or Sufism. You can practice spirituality on a yoga mat or through meditation. What a concept!

The very reason why New Age philosophy emerged in the first place was humanity's collective desire for freedom caused by the spiritual awakening of individuals across the world, especially since the 1970s. Today the number of people experiencing their spiritual awakening is expanding to the extent of it no longer being a rare, marginal phenomenon – becoming aware of one's stream of consciousness could soon become mainstream. And it started with the realization that spirituality doesn't have to be something that you are born and bred into, but indeed every person can choose his or her spiritual path.

The New Age perspective expanded Western spirituality to the extent of providing a wide range of techniques, teachings and Gurus to the delight of the spiritual seeker. This gave the spiritual novice the freedom to choose the teacher, path and belief systems of his or her liking, without having to disregard divinity completely (as an atheist would). And thus the New Ager was still following some discipline or another, and often experiencing serious limitations to his freedom, but at least he could choose a path and a teacher that resonated most with him.

This was all suitable for a while, but as individuals are awakening more to their awareness, many get weary of the rules and dogma of their Gurus. They become dissatisfied with the path laid out before them by a perhaps well-meaning teacher. To some students, spirituality becomes an impossible strive to get it right; an obsessive quest for self-improvement. To others it becomes a hobby, or even an ambition, yet remains worlds apart from other aspects of life such as work or family. Sooner or later, one way or another, the spiritual seeker becomes dissatisfied with the teachings offered by his master. The initiate hears something that doesn't resonate or feel good anymore, and the Guru falls off his pedestal.

This is the moment of the true awakening: The spiritual seeker becomes aware of her awareness. She enters her own 'age of consciousness', which ultimately will lead her to self-realization and mastery – and then spirituality is not only redefined, but also embodied. And so, many aspects of the New Age movement have lost their relevance as we move further into the 21st Century. The New Age has completed its valuable purpose of serving as a stepping-stone out of institutionalized spirituality into sovereign, self-lead, tailor-made spirituality.

Bringing Spirit Down-to-Earth

By now most of us who are on the "spiritual path" have heard it all: "Be grateful... Live in the now... Love yourself... Remain unattached... Focus only on what you want to attract..." – these mantras are the cornerstones of New Age spirituality. The question remains, if we know all these answers, then why do we repeatedly keep drawing the same problems into our lives?

Until these answers are personally experienced and applied to real life, they are nothing but black ink on a page. Shelves of self-help books are filled with catchy words, but when faced with illness, heartbreak, money problems and other real challenges, they grow pale and flimsy like governmental policy that flashes dramatically on the headlines of a newspaper only to dissolve the next day into piles of paperwork and bureaucracy – rarely reaching the streets, the homes or the hearts of people. Let's be honest, being grateful is bad advice to someone who feels deeply disappointed by life. Telling the person who just got his heart broken to simply "unattach" himself is not helpful. "Living in the now" can seem like a joke when one lives in a society run by the clock and where nearly every adult has goals to reach, deadlines to catch, and relatives to constantly pull one back into the past. Yes, there is deep wisdom rooted in each of these spiritual teachings; the key is to not leave those pearls of wisdom as dainty concepts stacked in the shelves of your mind, but rather connect to these tools in a tangible, visceral and sensory way.

Your spirituality is yours – it's private, it's sacred and it's a very personal business. It's between you and spirit (also called soul, divinity or consciousness, if you prefer). Therefore, do it your way, in your style, with your flavour and at your pace. What if spirituality wasn't some secret club to which you had to earn access by paying the price of denouncing earthly pleasures; consider instead, that spirituality could mean inviting your spirit to participate in your life – in *all* aspects of life. What if spirituality wasn't meant to be figured out or suffered through or even escaped into; what if spirituality could be fluid, organic and free; what if spirituality was as inseparable from your profane life as oxygen? What I'm saying is this: There is no need to choose between committing yourself to spirituality or to embodied, sensual life – you can have both.

If we strip off all the sugarcoating, the platitudes and the wide variety of techniques, what remains at the heart of New Age philosophy? What is the essence of any spiritual devotion? What lives on when the highly esteemed Gurus fall off their pedestals? What happens to the spiritual explorer, who perhaps is inspired by many teachers and religions, yet feels no inclination to follow any of them?

The spiritual pioneer bumps into *consciousness* – or crashes, because often this first encounter between a human and his or her consciousness is catalysed by a physical or metaphorical crash.

(R)evolutionary Consciousness

Consciousness, that awareness that expands beyond thoughts and even beyond emotions, is at the core of any spiritual practice. Consciousness is the pure element unattached to Earthly elements yet affecting them. It exists beyond time and space and is independent of the human mind or the physical brain. It is the undecorated truth, the spirit of spirituality so to speak. Consciousness is the starting point, it is the point of expansion and it is where all spiritual seekers sooner or later return. Consciousness is the cause and the effect of this spiritual evolution that humanity is going through.

The shift that we are lucky enough to witness (and create) is that of spirituality transforming, one individual at a time, from a structure of power into an experience of consciousness. Consciousness is the new healing. It's the new spirituality, and eventually it will be the new way to do business and politics and family structuring. Consciousness is in style. It *is* style. Like any real style, it's not a fleeting fashion but a timeless enigma that has existed patiently under the radar for eternities, and is floating into the spotlight when humans are ready for it. Consciousness does not depend on the temporary forms of religion and spiritual practice to exist (thank God!). Consciousness might dress itself up in spirituality, but do not mistake man-made spiritual practices for spirit itself – *you* are consciousness (also called spirit, God, divinity, soul…), and your spiritual practices are rather strange attempts to get back in touch with yourself.

Yes, consciousness will shake things up like any (r)evolution, but it will also act as the catalyst to everything exquisitely, perplexingly, preciously *new*.

Spiritual Freedom

To acknowledge the presence of divinity within every human means tipping sacred cows. It raises some provocative questions: Can spirituality really exist beyond ancient traditions, secret teachings, hierarchical structures and rigorous devotion? Can spiritual awakening and enlightenment be realized without the framework of defined and controlled spirituality? This book says: YES, it can; sovereign spirituality *is* accessible to anyone who is ready to choose it and allow it. I'm talking here about spiritual freedom – the freedom to connect to the divine directly, without the need of a guru, teacher or priest to act as the middleman.

The message of this book is very simple: The only difference between already ascended beings such as Yeshua, Buddha, Lao Tzu, Kuan Yin etc. and not yet ascended beings is that they have fully remembered, accepted and allowed the truth that they are divine. Ascended masters are not above other human beings, they simply realized their sovereignty before the rest of us (just like there will be others who will come after us). Ascension is the birthright of every souled being who chooses it. It is not a status or a position in the hierarchy of spirituality; it is simply the realization of freedom.

Archetypes of Ascension

For the purpose of this book, I will define spiritual awakening as becoming aware of one's spirit – or consciousness – and enlightenment as the moment when one's awareness has become so crystallized and clear that it shines into one's every aspect in full acceptance and self-love; enlightenment is the complete integration, wherein the human realizes and merges with his or her divine consciousness, thus transcending the illusion of duality. An ascended master is a being who has completed their journey of lifetimes on Earth. I use the terms enlightenment, ascension, freedom, sovereignty and self-realization synonymously in this book.

In the past, enlightenment usually meant that the ascended master crossed over and left the physical dimension at the moment of completion, mostly because human biology was not able to hold the sudden and intense infusion of consciousness. There is also another way to realize one's enlightenment, which has become more accessible as the energies on the planet are changing, called *embodied enlightenment*. In embodied enlightenment, the human integrates his or her divinity without death of the human body. This path of enlightenment is generally more incremental and thus less intense (but make no mistake, it will nonetheless require a complete dis-integration of the human identity).

Spiritual awakening is the moment or the phase when a person begins to ask questions or have insights about her existence beyond the human identity. In awakening, no matter how long it lasts, the human starts to expand her awareness, perhaps unconsciously at first, and later more purposefully. Awakening means stepping onto the path of enlightenment. It is a natural process that is ignited by the soul of the human in divine timing. While others can inspire or catalyse the awakening of someone else, it is ultimately the freedom of every human to either allow or postpone his awakening. This book describes some of the dynamics of awakening, and the shift into later stages of the experience of mastery and self-realization. Also the challenges within the context of modern life will be discussed. Enlightenment is something that ultimately unfolds beyond the limitations of time and space, yet for the purpose of this book, the phases of self-realization are presented in a linear fashion.

Since there are very few humans who have ever realized their enlightenment while staying embodied, not much is known about this exquisite experience, and even less has been written about it. Most of the information written about ascension comes from channelled texts, rather than from embodied humans. Yet humans who are enlightened and walking the Earth do exist, and I have met several such individuals. I didn't see a golden halo above their head, nor did they float in mid-air, or go around announcing how enlightened they are. They didn't appear different or special in any way that could be objectively defined or measured by the human senses. They had a depth and clarity in their eyes, and they were at peace with themselves. They were not powerful or all-knowing, but they were masters of their own freedom.

What is your mental image of an ascended master? The archetype of the ascended master is commonly depicted as a penniless man in white robes, who meditates in caves or mountaintops, and never loses his temper. The images of Merlin, Gandalf and Dumbledore spring to mind. Another common archetype is that of an avatar, a transhuman who has defeated death, gravity and hunger. But we are living in the 21st Century, and most of us don't relate to these archetypes. For me it has been helpful to learn that the ascended masters who have come before us were as colourful, unique and imperfect as any human.

For instance, there have been the rebels and revolutionaries, such as Yeshua and Osho, and their ascension was often bloody and dramatic. This archetype is depicted vividly in the movie *Braveheart*, and less vividly (and badly translated) in the Bible. Some were hermits who realized their ascension after lifetimes of discipline and abstinence, until they finally allowed compassion for self, like Gautama Buddha. There are the religious and serious ones, like Master Tobias and El Morya, who walked the path of devotion, yet chose to transcend all organisations and institutions in the end. There are the alchemists who searched for the elixir of life and eventually discovered the alchemy of the self, like Saint-Germain. There are the philosophers who tried to study their way into enlightenment like Kuthumi lal Singh, only to find enlightenment beyond all knowledge and philosophy. There are masters who found enlightenment by allowing their feminine nature to shine, such as Kuan Yin. There are masters who experienced abuse and disempowerment until they chose self-love, like Mary Magdalene. There are ascended masters who were priestesses and martial artists, scientists, creative artists, housewives and prisoners. There are masters who experienced all the colours of love until they found the freedom of true love and with it, ascension. Whether the path is religion, rebellion, silence, simplicity, alchemy, love, art or something else, every path is unique. There is no wrong way to enlightenment, but there is *your way* and it is yours alone to discover.

Returning to Self

I'm aware that some people consider enlightenment to be of such sacredness that only the most esteemed spiritual teachers should be allowed to speak about it. Others, who possess a more scientifically inclined mind, might wonder how anyone can talk about such a metaphysical concept with complete sincerity. And yet I do, because I'm an advocate of sovereignty and spiritual freedom. I find that writing allows me to catch the fleeting insights and inspirations that pass through the mind as swiftly as a shooting star.

My human self is writing this book in co-creation with my inner master. Although these words come from within me, I doubt that anything written in this book is truly new or original. Like any good writer, my attempt has been to weave age-old concepts together in a new way and to dress up timeless truths in an interesting fashion that is relevant to the modern reader.

One of the gifts I have been blessed with is an insatiable curiosity to explore psychological landscapes. There is an addictive quality to finding answers and gaining knowledge. I should know, having read hundreds of spiritual books, always in search of something I couldn't quite pinpoint. There comes a point in the life of a spiritual seeker when the answers are no longer enough; once found, the answers feel hollow. And so it happened for me: it wasn't enough to know about spirit; I wanted spiritual freedom actualized in a human body. For me, it didn't feel real to worship some distant, abstract and invisible God. Instead I made a choice to *embody* this newly found sense of divinity. I chose to explore what happens to divinity when it is breathed into the human body, and to explore what happens to the human self when it is touched by divinity. Perhaps divinity has been here all along, a spark within us and around us in every molecule – and the only real change is when our eyes and hearts open up to receive it. In an era where scientists are creating miracles by exploring how technology can merge with humanity, there are consciousness pioneers like you and me, who are exploring how humanity can merge with divinity.

Where have my explorations led me so far? The books that I read, the teachers I heard and all the twists and turns of my life brought me to a surprising place: back to my Self. Not to my human personality, but to a deeper, more intimate, yet formless self. One by one, each experience tore another crack in the shell of human limitations and false identities – despite all, and there was a lot, my body, mind and heart opened up. Like a spiral, the consciousness beneath my thoughts and emotions unravelled my perceived identity, until there was nowhere to go but to return to the core of the true Self. Another turn of the spiral dance. Every spiritual experience was (and still is) either a distraction, or a catalyst that drops me deeper into myself.

You can surely be inspired by the stories of others – indeed that is one of the purposes of this book –, you can take a breath of relaxation from your search by indulging in a moment of assurance as you allow the light of compassion or the humour of someone else's words light a warm flame in your heart. But when it comes to the real, deep truths, they are *within you*. Those unfold through your experiences; they come to life in your imagination and bloom in your heart. Yes, accept the support of a wise master, if it feels appropriate. Friends and teachers may even speak the very right words at the right time, but that doesn't mean that you can avoid yourself and your divinity forever.

So above anything else, this book urges you to go out into the world, to go within into the worlds of you, and then write your own bible. Write your own path, with your questions and your answers and then you will feel the veils lifting. Ultimately, nobody else can do it for you. You may be able to hold that illusion for a moment, that someone else can teach you your truth, but sooner or later you will expand beyond that; *You* are the key, the vortex, the channel, and the Holy Grail that holds the sacred mysteries of your soul and nobody can ever take that away from you. Other people may distract you or trick you into believing that you don't have a direct connection to divinity, but you can always come back to the remembrance that you *are* that divine wisdom within you, and therefore you are always connected to it.

From Self-Improvement to Self-Acceptance

This book is not written to satisfy the doubting mind or to help you create a better life. There are plenty of other books for that. This book is written for those individuals who have opened the door to the divine, even if just a crack, and are passionate about *embodied enlightenment*. It will not be everyone's cup of tea, but is written for anyone who is courageous enough to at least consider that spiritual enlightenment does not belong to the dusty pages of spiritual scriptures and legends, but can be *real* for real humans living modern 21st century lives. Will this book tell you how to attain ascension? No, because your inner master already knows the answer to that question, and because every journey is unique. But I will share with you what I have learned from my own experiences, and what my soul and many wise friends and teachers have taught me. I will share some of the things you can expect as a result of walking this path, and I will encourage you in finding your personal compass for this deepest and most daring of endeavours. I will share my perspectives openly, while remembering that the deepest truth can only be experienced – never explained by one mind to another mind.[1]

Although words can never match up to a real spiritual experience, the right words can act as a bridge between consciousness and the mind; as the translator that transforms something infinite, essential and everlasting into a temporary form or concept, so that the human aspect of ourselves can catch at least a glimpse of it. Yet I urge you to *sense* the words and to read between the lines. Feel into the energies of the various chapters in this book, sense the presence of those living masters who open their hearts and share their personal experiences with you. You will get the most out of this book by reading it slowly, because the messages are multi-dimensional,

---

1   In this book, the mind is defined as the human intellect, which is always tethered to the matrix of emotions and biology. The mind is a small, limited and highly programmed part of our consciousness designed to help us survive as humans, and that we often mistake as our identity.

and by allowing yourself to relax into the essence and the vibrations of the text.

This text deals with the invisible layers of life, the inner realities. The focus here is not to satisfy our human needs and desires (for example, the need to explain and understand), but to soothe the human self as it walks beyond its old concept of self. Spiritual awakening is never risk-free, and hopefully this book helps your human self to survive the challenges of awakening and walk through it with as much joy and grace as possible.

This book can serve as a frame, holding a white canvas, waiting to be painted by you. Your presence and your realizations are the paint that creates more expansion. This book also serves as a safe space, a special dimension where you can dive into stillness and listen to your own wisdom; and lastly, it serves as a mirror that reflects your divinity back to you.

I wrote this book on the premise that the best self-help tools always come back to self-acceptance – it's time to invite the practice of self-acceptance into the field of personal growth and spirituality. With that, I invite you to enjoy the reading experience, and wish that it awakens your imagination and tempts you into connecting bare and raw, in full brilliance with yourself, if you so choose. Let us inspire each other, while walking our own chosen paths in sovereignty and respect for each other. *Namaste.*

Part 1

Fasten the Seatbelt, Read the Fine Print and Set your Compass to Freedom

Elegant Chaos

Let's face it: Awakening is messy. It is a crisis – a synchronistically orchestrated elegant chaos. It is life out of control. Awakening is not a hobby or a cool lifestyle trend, although some certainly try to market it as one. Many masters have said it before: *Awakening is the simplest, yet hardest experience a human can go through.* Simplest, because it unfolds naturally (despite your best efforts to stand in your own way). Hardest, because it unfolds your true nature (and because you *will* stand in your own way). If you are treating awakening as a nice distraction from your complicated life, as a tool for success or a solution to all your problems, you will get disappointed. Sure, there are moments when awakening casts a glittering shimmer over your life like sprinkled fairy dust, but soon enough, you'll realize that it is also a potent elixir with highly explosive ingredients.

You might have stepped on the path of awakening with the innocent intention of improving your life, yet the purpose of awakening is not to remove the problems of your external life. Eventually awakening will make your life easier, but only after first unsettling everything within you. There are many paths to ascension, but they all include undeniable, irreversible change.

The Fine Print of Awakening

"Your problem is that your shadow is a bit - how should I put it? Faint. I thought this the first time I laid eyes on you, that the shadow you cast on the ground is only half as dark as that of ordinary people... What I think is this: You should give up looking for lost cats and start searching for the other half of your shadow." Haruki Murakami, Kafka on the Shore.

Nearly all humans live their life chasing the same ultimate goal: to feel better. In fact, most people going through spiritual awakening have stepped onto this path in hope of finding happiness. However, we must understand that every human is a multitude of aspects, each with their own agenda: For example, your mind and your heart tend to have very different ideas about how to secure happiness. This is one of the reasons why we have difficulties making choices – because it's not just one 'us' making the choice. Furthermore, we are to a large extent unconscious of these various aspects and their agendas. Until we start to awaken, that is.

When we awaken, we are becoming aware of the many different voices within us, all of them with different needs. We certainly are aware of the ego, which is our human identity and driven by the mind. Happiness, as defined by the ego, is a state of comfort and security and is usually created by the avoidance of unpleasant truths. Unlike true fulfilment, this superficial and fleeting satisfaction is nothing but a defence mechanism, a method to escape feeling our feelings in the now moment. It's both comical and tragic how terrified humans are of their own feelings! The reason why this kind of artificial or illusory thing called 'happiness' is incompatible with awakening is that in awakening you start to open up (to awaken) to *all* parts within you – not just the ones approved of by the ego.

It is natural and healthy to want to feel good, however, the easiest way to feeling authentically "good" is by allowing ourselves to feel whatever we are feeling in the moment, even, and especially, the unpleasant feelings. Being at ease with yourself is the natural result of awakening, but it certainly won't make your ego happy! The free master isn't continuously high on happiness; the realized master doesn't care too much whether she is "happy" or not in this moment because she sees a bigger picture, a deeper truth, a reality that extends beyond the physical world, and therefore can open her heart fully to life, no matter what is going on. The free master doesn't fear losing anything, because he knows that he exists beyond happiness, beyond loss; he exists *no matter what*. Awakening is about freedom, sovereignty, empowerment, integration and mastery, and it is so much bigger than mere human satisfaction.

Discussing this distinction between temporary happiness and real fulfilment is important, since a great many people turn to spirituality in an attempt to fill the void within them or to distract themselves from their own darkness. Yet embodied, real-life spirituality isn't about filling this inner void with happiness; it's about exploring the void, and exposing it to the light of your consciousness.

Suffering is by no means a necessary step in awakening. There is too much unnecessary suffering on the planet already and too much idolisation of suffering. Awakening is absolutely a way to free yourself of suffering. That being said, awakening does require change, and as humans we are biologically

31

programmed to resist change and to favour circumstances that we can control and predict. The more we understand the necessity and the dynamics of change (and the accompanying discomfort), the easier it will be to allow this process to unfold naturally. It is helpful to remember that experiencing discomfort does not automatically sentence us to a state of suffering: We can unlearn our programmed reaction to suffer whenever we feel pain, fear, sadness, anger or numbness.

In awakening, you go through such a profound and complete transformation, that it's difficult to comprehend its extent. Along with everything else, your priorities will change; you start to become aware of potentials and possibilities that you couldn't see or accept before. Priorities also change because metaphorically speaking, you are shifting the position of your inner CEO from your mind-intellect to your divine intellect. Generally, it means that your priorities will change from seeking comfort and security to expanding your awareness even if (and when) it feels uncomfortable, vulnerable and risky.

In awakening, you don't become "happy" – you release or integrate the things that have hindered you from living in your *natural state* of ease and grace. You might not be cheerful and smiling every day (though you might!), but unlike before, you will let go of resisting your current state. In awakening you will see that the answer doesn't lie in gaining more energy (more power, more money, more success, more attention, etc.) but in gaining more clarity. True peace comes from having the clarity to discern the essential things in life from the inessential, from the self-love necessary to choose the essential, and from the courage to let go of the inessential. If you are looking for a shortcut to fulfilment – that *is* the shortcut (alternatively, you could practice Buddhism for about one hundred lifetimes). Just make sure to read the fine print before you open that Pandora's box called awakening. And if you're already way into your awakening, I honour you deeply for your courageousness.

Why the Path to Enlightenment Casts the Deepest Shadows Over Your Life

~ The wider you open your eyes, the clearer you see the shadows. And the harder you look at the shadows, the lighter they become. ~

The reason why so many of us 'lightworkers' get side-tracked, lost or caught up in catch-22s on our way to inner peace is that the way to peace is through consciousness. And consciousness is not always pretty – paradoxically, it can feel anything but peaceful! Consciousness means awareness, and that means becoming aware of everything, not just the nice things. Awakening is not about being a lightworker; on the contrary, in awakening you come to face all the shadows within you – shadows that were hidden for a good reason. Ask any psychologist: Most humans are not ready to face their shame, guilt and fear.

Awakening is a fire-breathing dragon that burns everything you try to hold onto, that turns your world upside down and yourself inside out until every part of your false self has been ripped apart or turned into ashes. And yet, it has nothing to do with karma or punishment. Karma, the belief in reward and punishment across incarnations, is a man-made design (much like the concept of sin) that has been promoted by those in power to ensure obedience from the lower classes for centuries. Enlightenment is not a question of worthiness; nor is it a test to be passed. If you feel in any way unworthy of your enlightenment, let me ask you: Which part of you feels unworthy? Is that aspect really you, or is it just a limiting belief of your mind?

Awakening is that point of no-return where you feel a soul-deep, undeniable desire to bring all the stories of your aspects into resolution. It's an inner calling to write the last chapter of your 'Book of Lifetimes' and completing any unfinished business. Not because you need to redeem yourself or achieve the next stage in your spiritual evolution (spiritual evolution is not hierarchical), but simply to close the circle that started eons ago. It's about freeing every caged bird within yourself, even the ugly and the imperfect ones, so that you can then distil all those human experiences into pure wisdom.

Awakening is not for the faint of heart. It is also not for the cold-hearted. It is for those who are bold enough to open their heart 360 degrees and let soul's light shine through their every cell and illuminate every lie they ever told themselves. It is for those who dare to go to the darkest corners of themselves and the deepest depths to find truth. For those, who say: "I don't know how to get there, I don't even know what it is, but I am ready to return home. I am ready to return to the home of my soul and the centre of my being."

Every human experiences spiritual expansion in his or her lifetime. It's impossible to *not* become wiser and more compassionate through your experiences as a human. However, the embodied enlightenment experience that we are discussing in this book is a completely different game. The depth of the self-transfiguration is much more radical. Compare babysitting someone else's kid for three hours with becoming a parent yourself – that's how radical the difference is between having a spiritual hobby or even a "spiritual lifestyle", and truly committing yourself to self-realization. Awakening won't change your life to a slightly better version of your past, and it probably won't make you a better citizen. It isn't about learning a few more spiritual lessons, either; awakening means letting go of the limitations of your human identity (not because there is anything shameful about having a human ego, but simply because it's time to remember all that you are). For better or for worse, awakening is a radical act!

Not everyone has chosen to commit his or her life to enlightenment. Many have chosen a different focus in this life, for example to collect more experiences of being human and of playing in the field of duality. There is no hierarchy of spiritual superiority and no judgement on the part of source consciousness regarding these choices. Like so many things here on Earth, it's about timing: Because of this very special time that humanity is witnessing and creating now, the energies are supportive for a large number of humans to awaken; the enormous changes that are shaking this planet are making this era ideal for awakening – never before has awakening fitted so well into the historical context of humanity. Of course, you will know in your heart what *you* have chosen for this lifetime: Whether it is to begin your awakening journey, or to complete it and realize your ascension. In the end, it doesn't matter; enlightenment isn't exclusive, but will happen to every single souled being when that being is ready for it. Just remember, no matter how long it takes from a linear temporal perspective, awakening is a natural unfolding.

I've sometimes wondered, which is more painful: Being deep in the depths of hell unconsciously, or rising out of the depths of hell consciously? For me there is no obvious answer. Awakening is often portrayed as a blissful, all-positive experience. And yes, it is a magnificent experience, but it also comes with drastic consequences – the more aware we are of these potential consequences, the less we will blame ourselves (and others) when things do get challenging.

Once you have committed yourself to awakening, you will stand at the crossroads and face that same choice every day: Do I listen to my soul or to my human addictions? Do I choose awareness or fear? Trust or panic? Do I choose new, unknown joy, or old, comfortable habits? – You will face many difficult choices, because choice is how we learn about freedom, and how we learn about who we want to be when we are free. If you're anything like me, you will choose the ego many, many times, until gradually, it becomes easier to choose soul (that part of you that exists beyond the ego). And then one day, you realize there is no more choice, because it's so obvious what you actually want.

"Life shrinks or expands in proportion to one's courage." Anaïs Nin

Just be aware that what you call 'challenges' will come, and *it will be okay*. Celebrate them! They are appropriate, temporary, and nothing more than opportunities to make new choices. Often challenges are the secret doorway to your soul, that sacred doorway that has been mystified and religionized for eons. Yes, there might be some chaos and turmoil in your life, but it's not some random accidental chaos; it is tailor-made chaos that was carefully designed by the wiser part of you to release you from those archaic and utterly useless patterns. Your past is out of style, so don't cry too many tears when it crumbles into pieces. (Although I totally understand if you do cry.) Awakening is not challenging because you need to struggle or suffer your way into enlightenment; it's challenging because we haven't learned how to live without struggle and how to accept change without struggle. Being at ease with yourself in a world where everyone else battles through life can make you feel like an outsider and quickly pull you back into the struggle just for the sake of company; opening up in a reality that is based on walls, boundaries and limitations can make you feel unsafe. But the truth is, you can choose to enjoy life even in the midst of the challenges of awakening.

(Note to the reader: It is recommended to take your time when reading the text to breathe in the energies and to *sense* the messages. In the new energy, you, as the reader, are not just a receiver of information, but a creator adding your own consciousness to the text.)

How to Navigate Through the Dark Night of the Soul into the Dawn of Enlightenment

"Two roads diverged in a wood, and I took the one less travelled by, and that has made all the difference." Robert Frost

The question is: How do you navigate a path when you can't see the path, when the ground drops underneath your feet, when your reference points have shifted and your target is invisible? Clearly the mind, which has acted as your faithful map and compass in the past, won't do the trick. In this chapter, you will find out why navigating your way through life in awakening feels so *different* from how you've been used to steering your course. We'll discuss the pitfalls and traps that you might stumble upon your path, as well as the hidden doorways and short cuts available to you.

To start with, know that you have a personal North Star, a magical compass that points you in the direction of manifesting your deepest, truest desires. Of course, you always have the freedom of choice: You can follow the needs and wants of the limited human self or you can place your trust in your core self, the soul. You, the human, have the choice to not worry about charting the course because your soul is already in charge – if the human personality steps out of the way. Your divine self is saying: "I've got this, I'm steering; you just lean back and enjoy the ride." It could be said that this whole path of enlightenment is nothing more than letting go of the ego's addiction to control, and instead relaxing into the trust of your wise and masterful soul.

Placing your trust in soul doesn't mean that you become a passive puppet to some invisible ruler. It means that you place your trust in your infinite essence rather than in a temporary, fearful expression of you. Often our truest desires are buried so deep within our subconscious, that we have no conscious understanding of what makes us fulfilled (although we often think we do). Your soul knows exactly what you need and desire because she is your true core, your most authentic and wisest Self[2]. Your soul is the fulfilment of your dreams, the timeless completion of all your journeys. She is already enlightened. That's why she knows all the shortcuts to your real fulfilment. Enlightenment is the full realization of the wisdom that, despite all illusions, ultimately there is no separation between human and soul.

Beyond Linearity

Remember that time in your life when linearity was still a thing you could count on; when you operated from a fixed place and you knew where you wanted to be in five years' time and your target didn't constantly change? You knew what you wanted in the future, because your future was the logical progression of your past (unless you were one of those rebels who already before their awakening opted for non-linearity). I certainly miss those times when I could still see the path in front of me. A funny thing happens when you step on the path of awakening: the path vanishes, and so do all other paths.

---

2   The soul, that formless and eternal consciousness at the core of our being, doesn't have a gender or a bias towards masculinity or femininity; I simply refer to soul as 'her' for the sake of simplicity.

Linearity is a function of the Old Earth. Linearity allows us to dive into the experiences of physical reality, duality, contrast, cause and effect... Our experiences within the field of time-space allow us to feel emotions and physical sensations, and also to feel our individuality, our uniqueness within All That Is. It has been said that only a being trapped in the limitations of the physical (linear) dimension can truly understand freedom, and thus ascend. Linearity is also a program of the mind, designed to help us organize our perceptions of physical reality. Expanding beyond linearity is above all else an internal freedom.

However, expanding beyond linearity doesn't require us to become superhuman. A person who masters the art of walking on water in order to be the most powerful man on Earth, is the least free of all. Yes, he might have the ability to control the elements and to surpass the limitations of physical gravity. But what about his inner state? Doesn't the obsession to be powerful, to be special, and to be in control indicate a man who is still controlled by his fears? If he were truly free, he would not fear his own inadequacy, or resist his lack of control. Going beyond linearity is a matter of perception – not of power.

I use the term New Earth to describe the dimension on this planet where so many humans are awakening. We can tap into this dimension, which is right here, and thus expand beyond linearity by expanding the way we see, sense and interpret things. We don't step *outside* of linearity (imagine suddenly floating right into the sky because gravity no longer held you in place – a bit inconvenient, I would say); instead we see the illusion of linearity, while still operating within it. In the East, spiritual teachers call this illusion the veils of the Maya.

A person who can see through the illusion of duality and linearity, can also tap into their sovereign source of energy, called *new energy*[3]. I will get back to the topic of new energy in later chapters, but for now it's relevant to understand that in awakening, one of the many shifts taking place is expanding beyond linearity. This leads to some interesting repercussions. For example, the old patterns and beliefs that used to limit you, are falling apart and thus they no longer contain your fears in neat little boxes. Containment is very comforting for the human, as are limits, which give direction and a sense of control. Your true self might be jumping with excitement every time you loosen up your old limits, while your human facet is confused as hell. It's all part of the natural unfolding of awakening.

Updating your GPS

General Positioning System (aka the Mind) → Genius Path Synchronizer (the Soul)

This brings us to the topic of life navigation. Clearly, choosing freedom means that you no longer let other people's agendas interfere with your course of action. If it only were that simple!

---

3   New energy is a term coined by the Crimson Circle, meaning: "The next evolution of energy that allows the integration of duality, including our divine nature and our human nature. While the current energy is vibrational, new energy is expansional in all directions at the same time." Source: www.crimsoncircle.com/More/Glossary

The challenge that many of us face at this stage is that our old desires are no longer valid, but we haven't really "found" our true self yet and have no clue what we actually desire. Emotionally it feels like crossing a bridge to a brand-new territory without actually seeing the bridge.

When you can't count on logic and linearity anymore, you need a North Star that directs you towards desires that you may not yet be consciously aware of. In awakening, you cannot rely on the mind, because the mind operates using past experiences rather than future potentials as its directive. In other words, you cannot move into the New Earth from within the parameters of Old Earth. The reason why you can't see the end of the bridge is that it will be nothing like what your mind imagines it to be.

What happens on the awakening journey is that you're updating your navigation system from a mentally operated system to a soul-led system. Practically, this means surrendering your human will for the sake of your divine will. All the enlightened masters that I have talked to, have gone through this.

The North Star guided the three wise men to the celebration of the birth of Yeshua and a new era of consciousness. In astronomy, the North Star is a constant, unmoving beacon amidst an ever-swirling sea of stars, which is why it was used in ancient times to navigate unknown territories. It serves as an illuminating metaphor for your true point of orientation – your soul: It's the eye of the hurricane, the ever-present light that you can hold onto when everything is in a state of flux or turbulence; when you feel like nothing makes sense and nothing can be counted on, close your eyes, take a deep breath and feel your core. Look within to your inner sky and you will feel your soul, your consciousness, shining its unwavering clarity. This eternal part of you is always constant, while your experiences are like planets rotating around it.

The secret is that you don't ever get truly lost, because you're not actually travelling from one point to another. What is happening in the soul's journey through its human incarnations is that the human aspect, which is a projection of the soul, is expanding out of this core point of consciousness into different experiences. However, the connection to this constant and eternal Self always remains intact, even when the human aspect temporarily becomes unaware of it. This is called spiritual amnesia, and most incarnated souls spend countless lifetimes in that state of amnesia before choosing to wake up. The urge that spiritual seekers feel to return 'back home' is the deep desire to remember this central point within themselves. Just like the North Star, your soul is the constant point of stillness around which your experiences and aspects orbit; it's your true point of gravity.

Your soul doesn't show you the whole path, because reality is flexible, fluid, and constantly moving. There is no single, straight path to the future, because the future consists of countless potentials. Your soul can show you various potentials – including the easiest next step that you can take. On the New Earth, you create the second step by taking the first one; you are walking an invisible bridge that sometimes doesn't exist until you step on it. In awakening, your path only becomes evident one step at a time. In other words, *you choose your destiny*, and your soul will show you potentials that are most compatible with your deepest desires, as well as warn you against those potentials that could cause unnecessary suffering. Yet even with the expert guidance of soul, awakening will feel thoroughly *new*.

If your North Star doesn't seem to burn brightly (if you can't hear your soul voice, in other words), know that it is there every step of the way, just like stars shine 24/7 but seemingly disappear during the day. This connection to your soul, your inner master, will grow brighter and clearer as you learn to trust and communicate with yourself. If you're in that awkward in-between zone where you no longer rely solely on the mind to plan your life, but you're not yet fully trusting your soul guidance either, be patient with yourself. It can feel confusing and uncomfortable to say the least, but it's just a phase of transition. In the meantime, here are some reminders and practical tools to consider.

Useful Short Cuts for Navigating the Back Streets of Spirituality

1. *There are no mistakes, bad choices or wrong turns.* You probably will go through or have gone through a series of challenging experiences, and have made many so-called mistakes. They're not. The best way to know what the right choice is, is to make the wrong one. Perhaps you've even (unknowingly) created life-situations that gave you opportunities to make difficult choices. Nothing helps you expand your awareness and remember your truth like a difficult choice – especially, if you end up making what you later considered the "wrong" one. We've all experienced some form of failure, which is great, since failure is an essential ingredient of expansion. Once you become aware of your true

creator-nature, you realize that there are no mistakes; there are only creations and experiences. Giving up the regret will make it much easier to hear your intuition. (And you will probably need to release the guilt/shame/sense of failure a few times before your newfound wisdom sinks all the way into your subconscious, so don't lose hope if it doesn't work immediately.)

2. *All roads lead to enlightenment, eventually.* The only question is: How do you choose to walk the road? Do you want to take the (relatively) easy way or the hard one? Remember that you don't have to earn, deserve, attain or achieve enlightenment. It is the natural evolution of a souled being. In other words, you can stop worrying about whether to turn left or right, because any path you could possibly choose will bring you closer to your self-realization. The wise master within you will take care of the right timing regarding your ascension. This realization leaves you free to enjoy the view while you're walking the path.

3. Instead of steering your life according to questions such as 'what is the right thing to do', ask yourself: *what brings you joy,* and then allow yourself to receive it without holding back. If you had never sinned, didn't need to serve anyone or atone for anything, didn't need to earn, redeem, solve, or find anything, didn't need to improve yourself, and didn't need to fear anything, what would you choose? How would you start your day? What would you eat for lunch? With whom would you share your precious time? Sometimes we must remind ourselves that *life is our birth-right* – this means, you don't need to earn your earthly existence, because your worth is a given; your worthiness is an unconditional, unequivocal, absolute reality, even though it's tempting to forget that. Now that this is

cleared up, how will you enjoy your day?

4.   If you have chosen the path of self-actualization, *expect the unexpected* and assume that your chosen path will not look anything like what you think it will look like. Be okay with things not making sense. For me this experience of self-realization became much easier once I relaxed into the acceptance that I don't know what's coming.

5.   *Your path is a personal, individual endeavour* even if you are part of a spiritual group. Not comparing your experiences with those of others will save you a lot of headache, although sharing experiences without the element of judgmental comparison can be very enriching.

6.   *Don't rush the process.* Awakening, and especially the last phases of realizing your full enlightenment are all about allowing the process, rather than forcing it. You cannot rush your spiritual re-birth any more than a mother can rush the labour of giving birth. You might think that impatience is cool, but in awakening, patience can be the last saviour.

7.   *Don't be afraid of getting lost.* As a matter of fact, getting lost is part of the process. Becoming conscious of the fact that you feel lost is like a dreamer becoming conscious that he or she is dreaming; feeling lost is the precursor to remembering who you really are.

8.   *Start walking and keep walking.* And I mean this literally as well as figuratively. Walk to enjoy the scenery. Walk without having to know where you are walking. Walk without escaping your past or rushing into your future. Walk at your soul's pace. Sometimes the best thing you can do regarding your life-

purpose is to forget about it and just dive into life. Your divine purpose will catch up with you anyway; you don't need to hold onto it – it will find you. When you don't know where to go, take one step into any direction, and then the next, because that in itself will move the energies and help to resolve any stuckness.

In addition to these reminders, let's look at this topic of soul-navigation in more detail. We will cover topics such as how to move forward in non-linearity, how to communicate with your inner master, how to overcome doubt and how to get unstuck.

Unplanning Your Future

~ Releasing your goals means setting your future free. ~

You will be tempted to make plans and set goals about where you want to be in the future, because that is how you were programmed to function. This is very typical, but it's not very compatible with awakening. Many spiritual seekers give up their human goals only to replace them with the goal of enlightenment. But enlightenment is not a goal that can be achieved, or a destination that can be reached. As difficult as it is for the mind to comprehend this, enlightenment exists beyond linearity. That means beyond goals and destinations.

You can't think with your current awareness who you will be in a year's time, unless you want to be exactly where you are right now. In fact, the only purpose that goals fulfil, is limiting your future to a margin that you can understand with your present mind. In other words, you set your expectations for the future based on the past. Naturally, this isn't a problem if you want your future to be more of the same past, perhaps only in bigger quantity or faster speed. But if you're in it for real transformation, then sooner or later, you will have to accept that you can't fully understand where you are going, because where you are going is somewhere you've never been to before. This happens on a personal level in awakening, but it is also happening on a mass consciousness level because of this specific time on Earth. Humanity is going through transformations that are more drastic than ever before, and we simply cannot know where it will lead us.

~ *Sometimes you can't see where you are going because that place doesn't exist yet. That makes you a visionary and a pioneer.* ~

It's a great practice to let go of mental control on a regular basis. The mind tries to manage, control and fear life, yet there are better functions for the mind: Let the mind worry about minor details, like how to drive the car or how to walk down the stairs without stumbling. Leave the management of your life to your *wisdom*. If you cannot *not* make plans, at least be prepared to change them along the way. Treat plans as the best temporary direction for your life until a better direction becomes evident. Let plans be fluid and flexible, if you want them to serve you in these unpredictable times.

The Role of Life in Awakening

~ *Your human life is the biggest distraction to your enlightenment (but it's also the key).* ~

The question that all initiates sooner or later face is: 'If I let go of the mind's attempt to control my life, then what is controlling this experience? What then determines my choices?' In awakening, the mind will take a backseat as *divine wisdom* steps into the metaphorical driver's seat. Going beyond the mind without losing the mind requires an inner focus. Not effort, but a clear understanding of one's priorities.

Having gone through these doubts myself, here are some suggestions what to focus on while the natural process is unfolding in the background:

1.   Perhaps the most essential practice is to take a moment each day (or better yet, many moments) to relax into your beingness. By relaxation I don't refer to mind-engaging actions such as watching TV or reading a book, or to unconscious actions such as falling asleep. What I mean here is conscious relaxation, which refers to relaxing your body and mind while staying awake and without any outside stimulation. Basically this means simply being in your own presence and finding that inner dimension of beingness. It is a time-out of the external realm of constant doing. This so-called practice doesn't require any restricting labels such as 'meditation', nor is it meant to be an arduous discipline. In the words of Kim Eng, a modern master: "Take some time to be in the timeless realm". Take a moment of solitude, of no stimulation, to momentarily disconnect from the external dimension and to connect to your sovereign dimension.

Slowly, this sense of inner space will seep into your normal activities. Then you will fully *be* in your doings. However, first you must learn how to 'be' without the distraction of 'doing'. Doing here refers to any activity or act of thinking.

2.   In parallel to familiarizing yourself with the inner dimension of yourSELF, allow life. Get involved in the external dimension, called everyday life, without fear of being "contaminated" by it. Experiment with experiencing life directly, sensorially and sensually – without filtering it through the mind. Instead of analysing, appraising and overthinking everything, try to simply feel and sense each experience as it comes along.

When life requires you to do something, do it. Devote yourself to this earthly dimension with as much vitality as you devote to your spirituality. In fact, let go of the artificial belief that your life and your spirituality are in any way separate, if you haven't already. If you don't move to Tibet to become a spiritual adept but you're nonetheless committed to your enlightenment, then you must bring your spirituality into your life. Face each moment as it comes, no matter how imperfect or unspiritual it appears. There is no need to fear the physical reality when you know of the eternal link you have to your inner dimension.

Your inner zone is that centre that anchors all the aspects of you (mind, body and heart) to your true self, and your physical body is what anchors your consciousness to this material dimension. By placing your awareness to your existence in both dimensions, they become synchronized. Imagine that your core is like a song, and the more attuned you are to the song of your soul, the more your surroundings synchronize with its rhythm. The more you allow your soul and your human self to inhabit the same space, the more you are allowing embodied enlightenment.

~ Be where you are with your awareness, and what you need will come to you. ~

If you are ready to be an embodied consciousness right now (not ready to get there, but ready to *be* there) follow the key of your life and be present with your experiences. See your life as a canvas, and all your experiences as raw material for you to create art with. Your so-called problems and challenges are like particularly delicious colours of oil paint, and now you can apply your consciousness (your skill of painting) to create an art piece.

Once you have consciously committed yourself to self-realization, every single experience you encounter *will* bring you closer to the realization of enlightenment. It's important to remember this, because then challenges become meaningful nuisances rather than pointless obstacles that need to be overcome. Like an artist, you will come to view those challenges as additional colours that enrich your palette.

"Dance with whatever comes to your front door." Ascended Master Tobias.

Please know, that you don't need to go searching for answers: Whatever you need will come to you – so remember to be present to receive it. Just live your life, enjoy it when you can, and dance with whatever shows up at your front door, metaphorically speaking. The infinite now-moment, as cliché as it sounds, is the right place for you to be.

Unveiling Your Intuition

Intuition, which has also been called gnost, divine wisdom, knowingness or soul-voice, is ever-present yet tenaciously ignored by most humans. It is a highly personal compass attuned to your specific energies. If you feel out of synch with your inner guidance system, it means you have stopped listening to it such a long time ago that it has become very faint. Your intuition might also have become suppressed, because the people around you didn't honour your inner voice in childhood. The transition we go through in awakening of moving from mind-led living to soul-led living is challenging, because we live in a society that worships the intellect and trivializes intuition and feelings. One of the greatest scientists once said: "The intuitive mind is a sacred gift and the rational mind is a faithful servant. We have created a society that honours the servant and has forgotten the gift."

When we are in alignment with ourselves, our intuition is clear and we hear it effortlessly. Conversely, when we ignore our feelings and are out of alignment, our intuition grows fainter. Luckily for us, the soul never gives up her self-communication: When we stop listening to the subtle hints and sensations that our intuition is signalling, the soul starts to speak to us through emotions. The longer we ignore the emotions, the louder they become. Finally, soul will try to get our attention by communicating through the body (by manifesting illness, pain, extra weight or other symptoms) or by creating accidents or dramatic life circumstances. All of these are means of the soul to get past the filters of the mind and the hypnosis of mass consciousness, and to help us get back in alignment with our true self.

To get back in touch with your intuition, you first need to focus your awareness within. Tuning into your inner world is all about sensing rather than thinking. Start by listening to all your emotions and inner voices – not believing everything they say, but simply listening to these voices and emotions. The same flow that brings emotions to the surface, also carries your intuition to the surface. Emotions affect your breath and nervous system and are also affected by the breath and the nervous system. This is why conscious breathing is a great way to free stuck emotions and to start recognizing how the different parts within us communicate using our physical sensations and our breath as their language.

When we begin to open up to the intuition, we notice that the voice of intuition is often accompanied by the voices of our shadow aspects, such as fear. This makes it hard for us at times to discern between clear intuition and our ego-voices. These shadow aspects were created for the "protective" purpose of hiding our authentic self. Instead of denying or resisting the voice of fear, give it space to be heard. There is enough space in the universe of your being for both your intuition and your fear. Just be clear about who gets to call the shots.

In enlightenment, we eventually go beyond emotions into pure feelings that don't contain the judgment, duality or tension of emotions. Emotions are feelings that are tangled up in the web of thoughts and beliefs, whereas pure feelings are sensations without the polarity of 'good' and 'bad'. Emotions are appraised and categorized by the mind, and they have stories attached to them. In the awakened state of consciousness, feelings are a sensual and sensory rather than emotional experience. However, before we can go beyond emotions, we need to go through them. Most of us are incredibly thorough and creative in our ability to detach ourselves from our own feelings and emotions, yet we can't go beyond emotions by resisting and fearing them.

There are valid reasons why our own emotions feel threatening to us, and why we'd rather run away from emotions than feel them. What usually happens, is that we were born knowing exactly what we want and need in the moment. Then, somewhere in our early childhood, we were either explicitly or implicitly taught that certain feelings are good and others are bad. We were also taught what we should and shouldn't want. On top of this, most of us never got any advice on what to do with our feelings, and if we got advice, it was more harmful than helpful advice (e.g. "you need to control your emotions"). All of this affects how we communicate with the multiple parts within us. The conditioning from childhood affects how open and authentic we are with ourselves, and to what extent we honour and accept our own feelings.

In awakening, like in the process of therapy, we open ourselves to emotions that have been supressed for a long time. Thus, we may feel emotions now that are reactions to past events, and have nothing to do with our actual current life situation. And yet these projected emotions feel just as real as the non-projected emotions. The irony is that the more we resist our emotions, the more they grow (that doesn't necessarily stop us from ignoring our emotions though). Conversely, if we allow emotions to flow through us without resistance – even when it feels uncomfortable and intense – they will transform quickly. Therefore, the quickest way to integrate unpleasant emotions is to feel them, and *be* in their presence without doing anything else.

When I feel overwhelmed by emotions, I find it helpful to perceive emotions as intense energy or as body sensations, because every emotion also appears as a sensation in the physical body. When emotions are viewed and felt as energy, or body sensations, they don't get tangled with the thoughts of the mind, but are felt directly. Then the emotion doesn't stick to the ego-identity, but simply flows through the energetic body until it's released or transmuted. Whenever an uncomfortable emotion is present, it represents an unfulfilled need. Usually when we are present and acknowledge the emotion, it either evaporates or we get an intuition about what the emotion is telling us regarding our supressed needs. For example, if I'm having a conversation with my partner, and I suddenly feel tension in my stomach, I would then listen to the message of this feeling. These sensations give us information about our boundaries, about what feels respectful, safe and joyful to us, or what doesn't.

Having said all that, there is a way you can connect to the pure intuition that lies beneath the layers of thoughts and emotions. You can either ask your soul to show you the best way for you to hear your intuition, or you can try the following experience:

1. When you are ready, sit comfortably and close your eyes. Choose the safe space and tell your subconscious self that it is *safe* to open up to your intuition.

2. Take a few deep breaths, and simply observe any sensations that you feel.

3. Without reacting to the sensations, notice how your body

feels, observe your emotions, your thoughts and your energies in a space of non-judgement.

4.   Once you feel a sensation, ask it what it is trying to tell you and what it needs from you.

5.   Usually the first layer that we sense is the mental layer. The mind will be tempted to give rational answers to whatever question you have, and it is usually in a state of anxious rush. That's okay. Allow the doubts of the mind to flow through. Simply observe without judgment. If you feel resistance or frustration, simply allow those feelings as well.

6.   Now you can sink all the way through the thoughts and the emotions to a still, deep place within you that is very peaceful and clear. It's helpful to slow down the breath. The more relaxed you are, the easier it will be to find this clear space. Here you can hear your soul wisdom. You can now ask your inner master a question. Remember that the answer may come immediately, or it may come to you later, for example in dream state.

7.   If you don't have a particular question, you can ask soul to give you a gift. Imagine soul handing you a present, and see yourself unwrapping it. What do you see? This gift is a symbol and it carries a message for you, a message that is important for you specifically, in this moment. If you don't know what the symbol means, ask soul to explain its meaning. When you are ready, open your eyes again.

This soul-voice is generally subtle, simple, non-emotional and immediate. It never judges, and it doesn't push you or rush you into anything. It usually communicates through images, feelings, symbols, the imagination, sensory imprints and/ or simply through a sense of knowingness rather than verbal language. Your intuition is always clear; the only thing standing between you and your intuition are the filters of the mind.

Have patience with yourself as you practice using your intuition. Hearing your intuition has so much more to do with practice than talent. We have a tendency to think that certain metaphysical skills are bestowed upon the rare and gifted, but using intuition is as much about practice as playing the violin. Practice allows the re-organization of the brain as certain chemical connections (neural pathways) are stimulated and strengthened. The way to practice intuition is to continuously return to that place of inner stillness. Another helpful tip is to be playful with your intuition; seriousness often limits access to our intuitive self.

Discernment Is Worth Everything

Discernment is the magic trick that can save you from so much unnecessary pain and struggle. Discernment is closely linked to intuition. From all the possible spiritual disciplines you could practice, this is one of the rare ones worth learning – because *discernment makes all the difference* to how smoothly or roughly your spiritual path unfolds.

Discernment means recognizing what is essential and what is not; in other words, knowing the difference between the mental/emotional voices of your aspects (or someone else's aspects!) and the voice of your inner master. It's the ability to distinguish between something that is in resonance with you and something that's not. It's not about finding that one universal truth; discernment, as I define it, is seeing the difference between what serves you in this moment and what doesn't serve you, or the difference between your present, free self and an out-dated version of yourself. It's not about knowing the most realistic perspective (that is mental discernment and highly overrated) but instead, it's about having the clarity to see the dynamics beneath the superficial layer of reality. Discernment means seeing that higher, wider and more multi-dimensional perspective that never gets tangled up in the insignificant details and the fleeting untruths of the confused human aspects.

Discernment is so very important because a lot of people will try to sell you their truths, and ultimately you can only rely on yourself to know which truth resonates with you at any given moment. However, you can only be safe from other people's manipulation, if you don't let your own shadow aspects manipulate you.

For example, a book may be 'in alignment' with one person going through awakening but not with everyone. Don't be surprised if something resonates with you today, but seems completely unimportant in a year's time. If you are in doubt about whether someone's teachings are pure or whether they are laden with a manipulative agenda, pay close attention to what you are feeling. There are certain warning signs that usually indicate that a message is spoken by the ego of the speaker rather than their soul-wisdom: For instance, if you feel confused, small, powerless or start to doubt yourself after hearing the message, or if the message is judgemental... As a general rule, the more rigid, righteous, hierarchical and dualistic the teachings of a particular teacher are, the less supportive their teachings are to your expansion. Another easy way to spot manipulation is to notice whether the person in question is using power. When somebody is using persuasion and control, or operating in a hierarchical system, there is always an element of power play.

Perhaps you have even come across spiritual teachers who use subtle manipulation on their students without even being aware of it themselves. If something that you read or hear doesn't work for you, there is nothing wrong with you. It simply means, that particular piece of advice doesn't work for you. Leave it be and look somewhere else. Of course, sometimes the ego will resist hearing something that undermines its importance. Your soul will always communicate to you whether it's advisable to trust a piece of information or not, so just practice listening to your soul again and again, until it becomes second nature.

For example, an instinct can be a message from your soul or it can be a message from your biological, ancestral and programmed self. In either case, it's wise to be aware of it. One trick that helps me to discern between a 'biological instinct' and a 'soul instinct', is to connect with my heart. The heart-chakra is like a portal to the soul, and when we allow this portal within us to be wide open, the mind has a smaller chance of confusing us with its agendas. (Technically, all chakras are portals to our expanded consciousness when they are open. In fact, what opens a chakra is letting the light of our soul shine into that part of ourselves that the chakra represents. However, the heart chakra represents the sense of love, and when we open up to this particular sense, we have the easiest access to our core self.)

Remember also that things don't have to make logical sense to be real or valuable – let soul bring you the solutions and answers that your mind can't imagine or believe in yet. You will feel in your heart whether something is of importance or whether it's just distraction.

Doubt – the Culprit of Awakening

Doubt is a huge part of the awakening path. Sometimes doubt is the very catalyst of the awakening process: For example, when out of the blue, something within you starts to question things. You start to question more and more, until you question absolutely everything. And then you wonder why you are plagued by doubt. So, let's dive right into it.

The truth is, your knowingness is available to you. Perhaps the only reason why you doubt yourself is that if you didn't doubt yourself, a lot of things would have to change drastically in your life. For instance, playing the victim role is pretty hard if you live in full trust of yourself. Trust, of course, is the antithesis of doubt.

Perhaps the biggest reason why we have fallen out of trust with ourselves, and out of trust with Spirit, is that we believe we have done something wrong. How can you trust yourself when you have made mistakes in the past? But what if you hadn't made a mistake – ever? What is a mistake anyway? It's just a perspective based on a dualistic mindset. If you would go beyond duality, you would also go beyond the belief of mistakes. There would be no right or wrong, no good or evil, just pure existence. And if there was just pure existence, there wouldn't be mistakes, there would only be experience and expansion and expression. So why wouldn't you trust yourself?

Well, the truth is, that you do trust yourself. You, the angel, allowed yourself to dive deep into the harsh density of Earth, all the while being under the veil of forgetfulness because your soul trusted itself so *much* that it knew beyond a shimmer of doubt that one day you (its human aspect) would find your way back home to yourself, even against all odds.

Don't worry if you can't feel the trust yet, because it is there; you are temporarily pretending that you don't trust yourself, because somehow it makes life easier in the short term. For example, it's a lot easier to adapt to society and appear 'normal' if you listen to your mind rather than trust your soul-voice; start talking about your intuition and suddenly you are prescribed anti-psychotic drugs. Another reason why many of us hold back in terms of self-trust is that self-trust goes hand in hand with self-forgiveness. And *total self-forgiveness is tough – it's hard-core awakening in action*. You can see why it's much easier to doubt oneself. Of course, there is also the sheer gravity of mass consciousness, which makes it difficult to escape the matrix of doubt and limitation.

However, it is possible to let go of doubt, so whenever you are ready to trust yourself, simply choose it. And if you are not ready yet, don't judge yourself. Be patient; the doubts will naturally melt away as you start to remember who you really are. Remember also that you don't need to trust the whole world and your future and all of your aspects; if you just trust your wisdom in this moment, you will see miracles unfolding.

How to Get Unstuck

Life is not meant to be complicated – but it usually is. Chances are, you would be bored if your life wasn't complicated. However, if you're the exception and you really are ready to live life and awaken in a *graceful* way as opposed to in a rough and challenging way, then there is an alternative.

Whenever you feel stuck in any situation, remember: there are always many options, and there is always a way out. *Where there is consciousness, there is a way.* If you can't see your way out of a situation that you are ready to leave, let your consciousness lead you into a new situation. Your job is not to understand rationally *how* you are going to change your situation; your job is to know that you are ready to change the situation, to make a clear and conscious choice, and then to observe with curiosity (and without control) how the changes unfold. Before you know it, the old situation will have melted away, surrendering to your clarity and choice. That's conscious creatorship. It's about finding that delicate balance between not resisting 'what is' while consciously going in the direction of your joy. The trick to succeeding at this balancing act is to apply the 'AND' consciousness: accept 'what is' *and* allow change at the same time. It's okay to be the imperfect human and the wise master at the same time; you're not singular and you don't exist in only one dimension.

Perhaps you also need a reminder that suffering is not necessary. It's the most common path to enlightenment, but it's certainly not the only way. Although suffering has been a very popular path *to* awakening, it's not the definition of awakening or even essential to the process. It's true that suffering is often the catalyst for awakening, because suffering gives you real motivation to transform your life and eventually to transform yourself. Suffering can inspire the expansion of consciousness because the lower your vibration is, the more intensely you need to apply consciousness in order to feel good again.

If you are stuck in a state of suffering, know that on a deeper level it is serving your expansion, *and* at the same time, you can allow yourself to go in the direction of joy. The deeper you are in the vibration of suffering, the harder it is to walk in the direction of joy. You can start slowly and take one small step at a time. If joy seems too radical, go in the direction of relief: choose things that make you feel slightly better. Choose things that make you feel a little safer... Don't expect yourself to jump from a very low vibration to ecstatic joy overnight, or from a state of deep anxiety to overflowing love, because that would only make you feel inadequate and powerless. Joy is our natural state of being, but when unnatural things happen to us, like trauma, we don't feel safe enough to relax into joy; *joy requires a safe space.* That doesn't mean there is anything wrong with you; it simply means you first need to re-learn how to feel safe physically and psychologically.

However, suffering tends to lead to more suffering, and is a hindrance rather than a means to enlightenment. Even if you have experienced a miraculous flash of awakening in your darkest hour (which can happen), suffering will not bring you all the way to enlightenment. In fact, you can't fully realize your enlightenment before you let go of suffering. At some point, you will come to the natural conclusion that your suffering has got to stop. Emotional processing serves you up to a point, after which it will only be in your way. You will need to move beyond beliefs such as "no pain, no gain." They are not true (unless you really insist on believing them), and what's more, they are a huge distraction from your more joyful potentials. Do yourself a favour and walk beyond suffering in your personal life! If you don't know where to start, start by reawakening your true self-worth: No matter who you are, what you have done, or what has been done to you, you are worthy of the good things in life, the abundant, healthy, joyful, loving, kind, sweet and luxurious things.

If you feel stuck, it's also helpful to remember that you don't have just one chance in life, or two or three, but you have as many chances as you choose. It's easy to think that once you have chosen a certain path such as a specific career or a relationship, you are stuck in it forever, but it's not true. You could choose to be someone new every day, if you wanted to. Realize that any feeling of being stuck is ultimately an illusion.

The reason why some people say they will do things differently and then generally don't follow through, is that they don't want to change, not with the totality of their being. But if all parts of you were ready and willing, then it would be very easy to change direction. If you are trying to change a particular area in your life and it's not working, be very honest with yourself: Which part of you likes the way things are now? Why and how is this situation comfortable? What do you get from the situation, as it is now? Energy always serves you, so if something is present in your reality, it is there for a reason. Open your eyes, and allow yourself to see how. Once you are ready to see how an unwanted situation is serving an aspect of you, it is much easier to integrate and heal that aspect, so that the situation is no longer needed.

Another thing to remember is that the meaning of healing changes as you become more conscious. From a more expanded perspective, you don't need to be fixed, repaired, or saved because on a deeper level you always have been whole and pure. In awakening, the perspective on healing changes from meaning self-improvement to self-acceptance; for a conscious human, healing simply means integration. If you are facing mental or physical illness, it doesn't mean you are less of a master than someone who is "healthy". It simply means your human self is not perfectly balanced, which is the case for every person's human aspect; *humans were never meant to be embodiments of perfection*. The difference between someone who has realized her mastery and someone who has not yet stepped into mastery is that the conscious, embodied master knows she is the imperfect human *and* the wise master. The person who owns his mastery has access to a wider perspective, to that voice that remembers: "All is well, no matter what the situation looks like on the surface".

Simply remembering the fact that any stagnation or limitation is an illusion and, on top of that, a temporary illusion, makes it a lot more bearable. Remember also, that your path will get easier as you integrate wounded aspects. Sometimes it may feel as if you are going backwards in your awakening, although in fact you can't go backwards. It's just that expansion doesn't happen linearly but in waves and spirals. The good thing is that the further into your enlightenment you get, the less anxious you feel when you reach another low point of the wave.

Allowing Resistance to Serve You

Feeling resistance toward something doesn't mean you are on
the wrong path. As a matter of fact, resistance is an excellent
indicator of an aspect that can be integrated; resistance always
points to an opportunity of growth. This is crucial to remember,
because you will feel a lot of resistance on this path. Do not
push or mentally force yourself through the resistance. The best
way to deal with resistance is to have a gentle but persistent
focus, and a very clear choice about letting go of resistance.
Seeing every resistance as an opportunity for integration makes
this experience so much lighter. It's natural to feel resistance
toward all kinds of things that make you feel uncomfortable or
nervous – just release the resistance you have about resistance,
and it will get easier.

The Inevitability of Getting Lost

Almost everyone will feel lost at some point in his or her
awakening journey. The reason for this is that the old reference
points that we have used in life to make decisions and find
direction are no longer valid, and for a moment we drop into
a limbo state, an in-between existence where we have left the
matrix of our old life but have not yet fully stepped into our
new life of embodied divinity and mastery. This phase may last
five years, fifteen years or fifteen lifetimes. However, it's just a
phase. Perhaps you have disconnected from your old friends
but have not yet found people with whom you truly resonate
– the good news is that we are living at a time of collective
awakening, which means that sooner or later you will find
other (living) people with whom you resonate.

Another reason why you may be feeling lost is that you are losing your old identity and have not yet allowed your true Self to emerge. It's like growing up, when you are no longer the child that you once were and you still don't know who you will become as an adult. In other words, you are not only feeling out of sorts in relation to your surroundings, but also in relation to yourself. It is natural to feel uneasy about the uncertainty that comes with change, and awakening is the deepest, the most radical and the most all-encompassing change you will ever experience in any of your human lifetimes. It sounds dramatic because it is dramatic. The best thing you can do if you feel lost is to accept that this is what you are currently feeling, to breathe deeply and know that it will pass. It is also helpful to find other people who are in the same situation, because feeling lost together is much more fun than feeling lost alone.

There's a Fine Line Between Crazy and Free

In awakening you will continually expand beyond your old comfort zone. Not only is your lifestyle changing, but your identity, your beliefs, and the very workings of your mind are constantly shifting. In addition to feeling lost when you go through awakening, it is not uncommon to feel like you are "losing it". The line between transcending the mind and "being out of one's mind" is thin. There are many reasons for this. For example, both states (the state of awakening and the state of mental imbalance) are very unstable, and in both states the mind is losing its control.

What is happening in awakening is that we are expanding beyond old limitations, and on the surface, it can look very much like going crazy or having Bipolar Disorder (or some other form of mental imbalance). However, there are very clear differences between "normal" mental health dysfunctions and the state of awakening: First of all, awakening is a natural process. Much like birth, it is a natural crisis. On the other hand, mental imbalances are coping strategies that help us deal with difficult emotions and survive in extreme emotional or physical conditions. As such, mental dysfunctions are not natural or healthy, although they might be the best or the only option available to someone in a challenging situation.

Although both states are unstable, they are unstable for different reasons: Someone with a mental imbalance is unstable because their identity cannot cope effectively with a current or previous experience. In other words, the lack of stability is the result of being stuck in a trauma. In awakening, the lack of stability is the result of being in a constant state of intense transformation. This can be compared to the transformative, unstable yet natural phase of adolescence (although awakening is more extreme and happens on many more layers compared to the phase of adolescence). Another difference is that in awakening, the loss of control of the mind is a voluntary and consciously chosen experience, whereas for most people who "lose their mind", the experience is an unwanted reaction to mental suffering.

Having said that, many people going through their awakening do experience depression and anxiety, to name two very common "conditions", but it is useful to note that they play a somewhat different function in the awakening person. It is my perspective and experience that the depression and anxiety that appear in the awakening human will rebalance naturally, and eventually disappear as the person becomes more conscious and starts to integrate their shadow aspects consciously.[4] It could be said that awakening is the ultimate therapy, because one cannot return to their true divine Self without integrating and accepting their shadow aspects. In fact, the therapeutic aspect of awakening is why many people stumble upon this path in the first place. Whether mental imbalance is a cause or an effect of spiritual awakening, the more interesting question is: Whether awakening is a cause or an effect of healing? Perhaps a bit of both...

Pathless Woods

"There is pleasure in the pathless woods." Lord Byron.

There comes a time when you have the epiphany that the way to enlightenment doesn't always go forward, but instead this experience is about expanding into all directions, outwards and inwards, all at the same time. You even expand beyond the limiting perspectives of time and space. In other words, you step away from the linear path. Then, shortly after that epiphany, you have another realization: In fact, you are not moving anywhere, because the path is moving through you; your experiences flow through you while you – the point of consciousness – is always still. You will realize that *you exist* even outside the confines of time and space. When you stop viewing awakening (or life, for that matter!) as a constant chase and just allow yourself to enjoy the pathless woods, or better yet, the timeless woods, *everything you need comes to you.* And

---

4   This information should not be treated as a substitute for professional medical or psychological advice.

then time feels less like a prison and more like a backdrop flowing past you, the constant observer.

This realization that you are an ever-expanding, but unmoving, point of presence that attracts all the experiences you need for your ascension, will bring you great relief, because then you can let go of the search. When you choose to be present in your *body of consciousness*, this point of convergence, you can let go of the agonizing questions of where to go next, and instead let the events unfold around you in a graceful synchronicity. Or a chaotic synchronicity – it's really up to what you choose.

P.S. Enlightenment has been here the whole time; you don't need to pursue it. Now it's just about you being here as well – here in this moment, here within your own presence – and allowing it to catch up with you!

11 Signs of Spiritual Awakening

Every human is walking a spiritual path – whether they call it that or not – because each of us is Spirit in human form. However, only some of us have chosen this lifetime as the time to awaken to our spiritual self. If you felt attracted to this book, it is very likely that you're one of those who have. If you're not completely sure if this path is your chosen destiny, take a look at the list below and see whether you relate to the symptoms I have described. Some of these "symptoms" of early awakening balance themselves out in the later stages, especially the ones related to anxiety, depression and loneliness, because we start to integrate our wounded past and learn how to release stuck energies. Other symptoms, such as sensitivity and intolerance towards power games, tend to become more magnified as we expand our consciousness.

1. *The compulsive search for answers and meaning*

Being obsessed with trying to figure out where you came from (and why) is a sure sign of awakening. In awakening you try to find meaning in everything, and are utterly baffled by the fact that most humans can walk through life in serene ignorance of their own origins! Nothing exasperates you more than people saying "that's just the way things are…" – you want to know *why*. As you move further into the experience of self-realization, you eventually let go of the identity of the 'seeker', because you realize that even that identity restricts you. The more you find peace within yourself, the more you realize that making sense of things intellectually doesn't bring you enlightenment.

2. *Sensitivity*

In awakening you become increasingly sensitive (physically, emotionally and psychically), for several reasons: You become emotionally sensitive and more empathetic, because you become *aware* of energies and because you're expanding your ability to *sense* emotions (yours and other people's). You also become physically sensitive to a wide range of stimulants, because your DNA is going through a deep transfiguration. This could lead to illnesses and irritations as your body releases old toxins. Common physical sensitivities include allergies and food intolerances, as well as becoming sensitive towards noise, pollution, smells etc. You might start to sense energies from other dimensions, which could manifest directly as extrasensory abilities or indirectly as tinnitus or other symptoms. Ironically, your heightened sensitivity coincides with an increased intensity of life, since in awakening long buried emotions are bound to rise to the surface.

When people criticise you for being too sensitive, remember that what is actually taking place is you becoming able to feel in a world that is very numb, sedated and emotionally censored – the problem isn't your sensitivity, but the fact that the majority of humanity is detached from their own feelings. Plus, you're going through the most drastic change of any of your human lifetimes – you're allowed to feel sensitive.

3. *Intense dreams and strange sleep patterns*

In addition to you starting to remember your dreams more, dreams tend to become very intense as your aspects start calling for your attention and telling their stories at night. Some dreams are simply about releasing stuck energies, whereas other dreams contain important messages from your intuitive self. If you receive a prophetic dream that is scary or "negative", it is probably your soul giving you a warning so that you can consciously choose a different potential for your future. Nothing is set in stone when it comes to your future, but it's best not to ignore such dreams either. What you can do instead is to examine the difficult emotions that the dream stirred in you and to integrate those emotions.[5] You will intuitively know if your dreams hold specific messages for you and how to interpret them. The boundary between waking state and dream-state may also get more blurred as you awaken.

---

5   The process of integration is described in detail in an upcoming chapter.

I used to experience very intense nightmares for years (and still do occasionally), and the dreams felt so real that they affected my wellbeing and functioning in everyday life. I wanted nothing more than to run away from the darkness and the terror that I encountered in dream-state, but I finally learnt that the only way to stop the nightmares is to face the dark feelings (in a safe space) rather than run away from them. Eventually the nightmares did become less intense as I stopped resisting them and learnt how to create a safe space for myself.[6]

Also, your sleep patterns are likely to change. Ironically, the awakening human tends to need more sleep than someone who is not going through drastic self-transformation. I've met many awakened humans who suffered from chronic fatigue during their awakening. Naturally, everyone's experience is unique.

You might find yourself waking up in the middle of the night and craving naps during the day. Sometimes you will wake up in the morning feeling like you've worked all night long, or wake up with strange aches all over your body. I have experienced intense sweating, being woken up by thirst, and a sensation of burning during sleep as if I had fever, despite having normal body-temperature. These symptoms are to be expected especially if you have made the choice to integrate your light-body; the body burns and releases old energies while you sleep.

Sleeping is a very active time for the awakening human when much of the sacred alchemy takes place. My recommendation: Sleep in nature or in the countryside once in a while; the silence

---

6   I describe this process in the sub-chapter *Alchemizing Fear.*

of nightly wilderness can be really rejuvenating. If you have a partner, try also sleeping in your own company sometimes. Drinking a lot of water during the day and taking a few conscious breaths before going to sleep will also help your nervous system to balance.

4. *Deep sadness and depression*

As mentioned in the previous chapter, not everybody going through awakening will suffer from depression, but it is very common. Another related symptom is deep sadness that might appear unrelated to life events. Most of us who are awakening have no concept of how grand a transformation we are going through. It's probably easier not to be aware of its incredible scale and depth. When we choose self-realization, we also choose to end our cycle of human lifetimes and basically say good-bye to our experience of being human. Even if this is our desire and choice, we will feel a deep sadness; anybody who has let go of a lover knows the feeling. But instead of releasing one relationship, in self-realization you let go of hundreds of lifetimes, karmic ties and old identities.

When I was just starting to awaken, I went through a phase of deep depression. Luckily, I evaded any pills, since in addition to being addictive, psychotropic drugs have some serious side effects[7]. The depression experienced in awakening usually has to do with the loss of passion, the disconnection from other people, the difficulty to relate to other people, and sometimes it's simply a consequence of the exhaustion and confusion of awakening. Often when we start to awaken, we create

---

[7]   If you are using psychotropic drugs and want to stop, it is safest to do so gradually (and consult with a psychiatrist).

an energetic shell or bubble under which we hide. This is a natural response and often appropriate for a temporary period, however, it also makes us feel alienated and separate from the world around us. Eventually we learn how to be safe without hiding from other people and from life.

5. *Existential anxiety*

When you start going beyond the old limits of your mind, you start to wonder where, how and if you exist beyond the mind. This can trigger some serious existential anxiety. The answer that will relieve you from that anxiety does not come from the mind. It comes from feeling your soul-connection, whether you feel it through creativity, love, sensuality or directly through sensing your soul. For me the existential anxiety naturally faded away as I became more grounded in my body and started to consciously communicate with my true Self. Related to this is fear of death, which every awakening human will face at some point. If you want to explore this topic more, you might want to participate in the DreamWalker Death Transitions School[8], or read literature written by humanistic existential psychologists, such as Rollo May or Irvin Yalom (see *Recommendations*).

6. *Homesickness*

Homesickness, loneliness and feelings of not belonging are very common, especially in the earlier stages of awakening when you start to notice that your desires are different from those of most people. At the deepest level, this homesickness is a

---

8   You can read about it here: www.store.crimsoncircle.com/left-menu/ advanced-studies/advanced-studies-workshops/dreamwalker-death-transition-schools.html.

longing for your human self to connect with your soul and vice versa, because soul is your eternal home. Something that can alleviate this pain on a human level is finding like-conscious humans with whom you can be yourself and who understand what you're going through.

7. Longing for a soulmate

This feeling is similar to the previous one and stems from a desire to re-connect all the dispersed parts of yourself, especially your masculine and feminine aspects. Whilst it is possible that you have made an agreement before birth to meet another soul in this incarnation and create something together with them, a soulmate is never a replacement for your connection to your soul! Self-realization is first and foremost a path of sovereignty, which is why many of us go through it solo. Just remember that whenever you feel an intense longing for that soulmate, you are always also longing for a part of *yourself* that you have forgotten about. Of course, sharing love is one of the best reasons for coming to Earth. Just beware of not replacing your relationship to yourself with some other relationship.

8. Going beyond the mind

In awakening, the concept "I think, therefore I am" goes right out the window. You become curious about what exists beyond the human mind. In fact, you start to get headaches from too much thinking. The mind is a sense, a way to perceive the world, but like all human senses it has its limitations. However, the answer doesn't lie in controlling the mind, but rather in opening up to new senses (new ways of experiencing reality). You could, for example, perceive life through the lens of imagination, creativity, love, or timelessness. These are examples of senses that are not limited by the boundaries of the mind.

9. *Intolerance for power-games*

Despite everyone complaining about power-games, most people wouldn't be able to live without them. This is because most relationships contain power dynamics and letting go of power-games altogether would mean letting go of many relationships. And yet, in awakening our priorities change and we learn that we can't have true freedom of Self without letting go of our addiction to power. It is not uncommon for people who are awakening to have a challenging relationship to authorities. Compared to humanity's recent technological developments, it is astounding how inept humans are regarding the most basic social skills, such as how to interact with others without being abusive or manipulative. Stepping out of power-games is a huge deal, and it may take a lot of patience and practise for the awakening human to take that bold leap.

10. *Constant and complete change*

In awakening, you go through transitions and changes on so many levels that you're no longer able to keep track with your own changes, because *nothing* is constant. Just remember, you're not going crazy, and there's nothing wrong with you.

11. *Multiple perspectives*

When you awaken, you become aware that everything happens

in countless layers rather than straight lines. Instead of perceiving life through a narrow tunnel, you start to perceive things as if your perception was a diamond: You start to see any given event, person or phenomenon through hundreds of facets. It's as if most people perceived the world two-dimensionally but you had 3-D vision.

This is why communication with other people is difficult even in awakening: You might see their perspective (the 2-D perspective) but they might never be able to see all the perspectives that you do. It's natural to feel overwhelmed by the complexity of everything and frustrated or envious of humans who are blissfully unaware. When you get overwhelmed by the complexity of all the different perspectives that you are now able to perceive, keep returning to the wisdom of simplicity: Yes, there are many, many layers to this thing we call 'reality' and these layers are intertwined in such complex ways that our minds could never comprehend all of it, but in the end, everything that really matters is simple.

I now invite you to take a deep, luxurious breath and accompany me on a journey through the pathless woods of awakening. Part 1 focused on *how* to move through the experiences of awakening. Part 2 is about *what* the experiences are that you're likely to encounter in those mysterious woods.

Part 2

What to Expect On the Way to Enlightenment

A Puzzle in Pieces – or a Miracle in the Making

Awakening is like throwing all the puzzle pieces of your life in the air, and then watching them fall into all the wrong places. Hardly anything initiates more questions than the experience of awakening; indeed, so much about this journey is 'puzzling'. Although awakening is a highly personal and unique experience for each person, there are some common characteristics that can be discussed for reference and clarity, as I have done in the following chapters.

The Catalyst

"The most beautiful thing we can experience is the mysterious. It is the source of all true art and science." Albert Einstein

This is the phase when the puzzle image of a neatly organized life explodes. Something happens that is so shocking, surprising or "wrong" that it draws your attention and briefly awakens you from your slumber of blissful, boring, predictable ignorance. Not everyone who experiences trauma experiences spiritual awakening, and not every awakening human experiences trauma. Trauma just happens to be the most common catalyst for awakening. For whatever reason, you begin to ask questions you somehow never thought of asking before and you notice things you didn't notice before.

So, there you are, trudging along daily duality when something catches your third eye. A book, a person, a sentence, or perhaps a breathtakingly beautiful scenery… Whatever it is, suddenly you see something strange in the midst of your clear-cut, black & white reality. You are very familiar with all the shades of grey, but something deep within you tells you there is more to life than this. Of course, in your imagination, in your heart of hearts you've dreamt about colours, and for the shortest instance you think you even see a glimpse of colour on the horizon. You tell yourself not to be ridiculous, that this thought is too wild to be taken seriously, and so you put more effort into focusing on that black & white life.

However, once you start asking questions, you can't un-ask them. You might not yet see beyond the veil, but at least you're aware that there is a veil. The human believes it is the only reality, the only dimension of your existence. It believes in borders and limitations and separateness, it believes in edges and in forms. Edges, forms and limitations are real, there's no doubt about it – however, what so many spiritual teachers are trying to convey is that they are one reality amongst countless other ones.

Every person is an entire universe. What you see of another person (and what he/she generally sees of his/her own self) is just one snowflake at the tip of an iceberg. We don't live in the outside world; we interact with it. We live our reality from within our perspective. You never leave you – but you can forget about the iceberg beneath the surface of your awareness to the extent that you feel completely disconnected from your inner dimension, the dimension of your true Self that is bigger than the universe. Because you are a free, sovereign being, you can always choose to change your perspective, that lens through which you view the outside world and the inner world. Adaptability makes us forget to see things from a wider perspective. We learn to take things for granted: "This is just the way it is, I'm nothing more than a little snowflake". When we begin to awaken, we begin to question everything. We start to expand our perspective, to try out different belief systems, and we start to question the realness of reality. The catalyst, in whatever form it appears, crashes (or glides) into our reality rather like Titanic into the iceberg. The effect is that we become aware that there is an iceberg; below the surface of our awareness there is something big, dark and mysterious – and perhaps wonderful, too.

The Matrix Cracks

"There is a crack in everything, that's how the light gets in." Leonard Cohen

Another way to describe this phase of awakening is that you become aware of the matrix. You become aware of this magnetic network, energy field, mass consciousness, this psychological spider-web that holds society together. It consists of norms, rules, perspectives, and belief systems. It is a type of mass hypnosis – not the conspiracy theory-type, but simply the effect of unconsciousness; a set of thought patterns that allow humans to experience limitation and contrast. This field is what holds the Old Earth reality together. This network supports us as long as we want to act within a set of limitations. It provides security and predictability. However, in awakening you start to become aware of this mass consciousness, and slowly you begin to explore the edges of this matrix. You are so curious about your true nature that you occasionally look outside of this field in search of new answers. You have played in this field of polarity, in the duality landscape, for so long that you feel ready to explore what lies beyond it. Awakening is not about being different out of self-importance or rebelliousness, but you will be different if you choose freedom in a world where being satisfied with limitation is the norm.

And so the journey begins. Expansion is an inside-out business: it starts from your core and grows with each experience. Not just through important or successful experiences, but through *each and every experience*. It's like a spiral: You may come back to the same experience a thousand times, and with each twist of the spiral you move through the experience from a new, "higher" point of perspective. Don't assume that just because you've learnt something, you won't be learning the same thing a dozen more times, each time in a different way or from a different perspective. The soul loves to expand, for with each experience of the human, it collects a drop of precious wisdom.

In your awakening, you will start to see lots of messages and hear about all kinds of spiritual tools (you will even find some in this book). Remember that tools are only tools; the right tools can point you in the right direction, but you still must go through the experience to embody it. Don't give your power away to things that are outside of yourself, such as astrology, channellings, tarot cards, crystals etc. These tools can be useful and fun, as long as you always ask your highest truth: "does this resonate with me?" and then dare to be radically honest with yourself. The best messengers are the ones that reflect your truth back to you.

In this phase you are so absorbed with awakening that you probably are a bit out of touch with your human life. At this stage of awakening it is typical to be obsessed with finding as much new information as you can about spirituality (which, thanks to the Internet, can be an overwhelming amount). You look up to the stars and to the edges of the universe for answers, but soon enough your attention will be pulled back to your human life. The moment you throw that passionate question, "who am I?" into the dimensions, an unravelling process is initiated. Awakening is not about gaining or achieving anything, not even more wisdom. You have done that for many lifetimes already. No, the real issue at hand is the peeling away of all those layers of illusion (although in some cases it would be more accurate to say that those layers of protective illusion are being *ripped* away) – which brings us to the second phase of awakening: the deconstruction of the ego.

Reality Out of Spin

"Chaos is nothing more than disrupted patterns." Adamus Saint-Germain

The next phase of awakening can be summarized as releasing your attachments and losing control. The loss of control is the result of you having started to dismantle the layers of hypnosis, the overlays of conditioning, the karmic patterns, your defence mechanisms and the gravity of mass (un)consciousness that used to feed the illusion of order. You probably know the common expression 'the dark night of the soul'. It refers to this stage of awakening (that lasts a lot longer than one night) when you are aware enough to ask questions and to realize your lack of awareness, but not yet aware enough to hear, or believe, the answers. You are aware enough to realize your own mortality, but not yet aware enough to know with deep, unshaking certainty about your soul's eternal existence. It's a phase of unfamiliar discomfort, existential anxiety and is often accompanied by a kind of spiritual depression or intense bursts of anger. Deconstruction of the ego (i.e. your life falling apart) is a natural and to some extent unavoidable part of the awakening process.[9]

Death, Divorce, Disease: When the Walls Crumble

"Every nature, every modelled form, every creature, exists in and with each other. They will dissolve again into their own proper root. For the nature of matter is dissolved into what belongs to its nature." From

---

9   The 'ego' here is defined as the limited self-concept of our human aspect, which consists primarily of the mind.

the Gospel of *Mary Magdalene*

Awakening doesn't have to be dramatic or disastrous – but if it is, there is a reason for it. The disenchantment and all that other drama is actually just about *disconnecting* from old patterns, and that can be an easy process *if* you are brave enough to let go of the old voluntarily.

In this phase you begin to disconnect yourself from the gravity of Earth – not the physical gravity, but the emotional, mental and psychic gravity. This means releasing all the energetic ties that somehow limit your freedom. For example: Releasing your past (what has been called "karma" but really just means unresolved issues), your spiritual family, your ancestors, the hypnosis of mass consciousness, as well as any belief systems about duality. This disconnection or releasing happens naturally, without any need for planning or controlling the process, so that you can reconnect on a deeper level to your sovereign domain and to your true Self.

The purpose of this disconnection process is not to escape the physical plane or to redeem yourself of the sinful pleasures of the flesh, but to create space within your physical existence for your divine Self.

The reason for things falling apart (or blowing apart) in awakening is to allow you to open up to all the dimensions of yourself. Imagine that your energy has been very tight and full of knots, instead of freely flowing. Now you are awakening and want to integrate the light of your consciousness into your physical body, but there is no space because your muscles are tight, and your heart is tight, and especially your mind is tight. In order for you to fully embody your consciousness, you have to open up and create space for the new to enter. And sometimes things break or fall apart in the process.

When I talk about disconnecting in this context, I don't mean detaching yourself emotionally from friends and family, or putting walls between yourself and others. Rather, it's about disconnecting yourself from old patterns and old dynamics of energy exchange between yourself and others (or yourself and your aspects). Having said that, these are deep changes that will affect your relationships.

To use an analogy, imagine a cast of actors who are performing a stage play. Everybody has learnt their roles and their lines, and suddenly, during the performance, one of the actors starts to improvise instead of act according to the script. As you might guess, the other actors are not happy about it: They are put on the spot, and now they have to be spontaneous and creative and authentic; they have lost control. Similarly, when one walks into a family dinner, and after decades of adapting to the "family script" and playing a certain role within the family, brings a new version of themselves to the table, it is likely to cause distress. Everybody feels uncomfortable, even when the new version is much more balanced than the old one. The fact is that we are not the only ones attached to our old identities and roles – the people in our lives are also attached to the identity that they have associated with us. This is one of the reasons why changing ourselves is so challenging: We cannot truly change ourselves without also changing our relationships.

Sometimes taking physical distance from your friends or family, at least temporarily, and in some cases permanently, is necessary or useful, because you are stepping into a completely new way of energy management: instead of trading or stealing energies from others, and letting them steal your energy, you are becoming conscious of a new dynamic of human interaction that is not based on power and transaction, but instead your interactions are based on your connection to your consciousness. At first, it's very confusing, because the people around you sense the change that is taking place within you but don't understand it, and perhaps you don't understand it completely either. The best thing you can do in that situation is to be constantly aware and honest with yourself regarding what feels right for you, and then follow that feeling. Sometimes our surroundings adapt to the new version of us, but sometimes they don't. Then it's up to us to make the choice: do I stay or do I move into a new direction? There is no right answer, but the more honest you are with yourself about what feels right for you, the easier it will be for everyone.

Humans like patterns because patterns mean control, which in turn means comfort for the human self. Yet patterns are very incompatible with authenticity, newness or with being in the moment. What we must understand, or at least accept, is that awakening is not just another pattern. It's the choice of letting go of patterns altogether. It's the choice of stepping in and out of certain behaviours and belief systems according to when they serve us, rather than being locked into or addicted to them. This is why freedom is a double-edged sword: free of limitations also means free of control.

Whether your personal "dragon" manifests in the form of difficult relationships or whether it's disease or the death of a loved one, or something else, it is very easy to get stuck at this stage of awakening. Instead of processing that issue, just allow the energies to move. Processing your problems has the tendency to keep you stuck in the mud; it keeps you spinning in your patterns, because there's a seductive pull to the past. Do whatever it takes to become aware of those old patterns and then release them. If letting go of patterns altogether feels too radical, at least try some new ones. Remember that energy needs to constantly move, change, flow and expand; it wasn't designed to stand still and it will explode if you don't allow it to be in motion. Divorce, disease, or any form of loss are just examples of previously stuck energy starting to flow again.

Ultimately it always comes down to the choice: will you let a distraction, such as a difficult relationship, come between you and your divinity, or not? The problem is never the difficult relationship (or whatever form your dragon takes) in and of itself. If your relationship, or your health or your career is falling apart, remember that this is an opportunity to make new choices and become clear about your priorities. Many parts within you will resist the change, because you've never done that level of releasing before, at least not while being an embodied human. This inner discomfort and resistance isn't a sign that you should give up and avoid change, but rather it's the time to be very compassionate with yourself. You can be sure that soul is guiding you into the right direction, and you will create situations in your life that help you to disconnect from your limited self in one way or another. It's common to be self-absorbed when you go through this phase, because you are finally starting to turn inwards in a world that is very outward-oriented. It doesn't make you selfish; it makes you self-full. You are gradually cutting yourself away from your old energy sources so that you can find your own, sovereign energy source

– your consciousness.

This falling apart of your old reality is, of course, the alchemy of enlightenment. This transfiguration is not about improving yourself or perfecting your human identity or even about processing your past self; you don't need to process all your so-called "bad" and wounded aspects. Awakening is an alchemical process of collecting all the elements of what you are and have been and could be and throwing them into a cauldron to be transformed into their highest potential. The reason why most people experience deep emotional and/or physical challenges in this stage of awakening is to trigger their dark (meaning unconscious) aspects, so that these rise to the surface of their awareness and can then be integrated. Not mentally processed, but whole-heartedly accepted, as they are. Integration is the deepest form of healing. In integration, you bring your past into the now for healing, and for letting go. Enlightenment is the result of surviving your own darkness, and ultimately, your own mortality.

Winds of Change (and Sometimes Hurricanes, Too)

~ *The harder you push, the sharper the cracks of your breaking ego.* ~

Awakening is incredibly humiliating. It's not politically correct, not always healthy and as Adamus Saint-Germain put it, it's not polite. You'd think that rediscovering your divinity is exalting, which it is in many ways, but it's also the death of your ego. In awakening the ego, that you have used to shield your soul from the world, starts breaking. Like an earthquake, awakening brings you out of balance and shakes things up. The very foundations on which you have built your life (namely your identity) will crumble under your feet. The matrix in which you have lived and in which things make sense begins to dissolve before your eyes. Suddenly order is nothing but a house of cards. And with every crack of the ego (and sometimes of your heart), the light of your soul shines brighter into the world.

The more you try to hold onto your ego while awakening, the more humiliating it will feel. The easiest way to deal with the ego (if you are truly going for enlightenment) is to allow it to gracefully crumble. The more challenging, yet popular, way is to hold onto the ego kicking and screaming, but the end result will be the same. Ask yourself: "What is my priority – a pretty life, or total freedom?" It's not an easy question to answer, but a necessary one if you're on this path.

What if balance had nothing to do with outer stability? What if true balance meant that the complete unhinging of order as we know it didn't affect you because of your *inner* stillness? What if true balance meant that you were so intimately connected with your soul, so centred in your own truth that you didn't need the gravity of normalcy to stabilize you but instead you could glide from one dimension to the next, rooted and grounded whenever you chose, yet light and free enough to float into new unknown experiences at will? In awakening, the winds of change will blow hard in your life, but sooner or later you'll discover the master-Self that always resides in her sovereign domain where no wind can throw her off balance. Sure, the rough winds might still affect the human part of yourself, but the great news is that there is another part of you that never loses stability because it was never invested in the human identity to begin with. You see, this part of you doesn't fear losing control, because it never believed in control in the first place and it definitely doesn't believe in fear.

It is understandable, but useless, to want to control your awakening. So what, if you lost control – would the world fall apart? Try it once, and see what happens. Probably *your* world will fall apart, to some extent. But let me ask you a very bold question: So what? Maybe it's time for things to loosen up. By the way, "so what?" is an incredibly useful question to ask yourself on this path; it can really help to free that victim mentality or an overly serious attitude: *So what if somebody doesn't like you – why should they be obliged to feel a certain way about you? So what if you don't have any money in your account – create some more! So what if nothing makes sense – in fact, it might even feel like a relief to not try to understand everything and simply enjoy life instead. So what if you lost your job – now there's space for something new to come into your life. So what if your heart is broken – at least you can feel again. So what if you die? It's just the human body that dies, what's you about you will exist no matter what...* Are these questions reckless? I'd say that asking yourself these kinds of questions is incredibly liberating for the mind, because you are no longer in a state of forced pretence. Interestingly, the mind is somewhat ambivalent when it comes to control: it's absolutely addicted to control, but at the same time, it needs occasional liberation to function properly. Much like a computer, it needs to shut down occasionally. I'm not actually encouraging any reckless behaviour here; I'm simply saying that if you learn how to loosen up, especially on a mental level and preferably without substance abuse, you'll have a much easier time with this process.

Somewhere along the path of awakening, perhaps shortly after contemplating your own death and the impermanence of your human identity, you start to breathe. I mean consciously, passionately, totally, with the whole capacity of your lungs. Perhaps it takes a trauma or a disaster, but eventually you will start living life from breath to breath, rather than from goal to goal. And that's when inspiration can flow into your life. There is a deep connection between the breath, the spirit and your passion for life. And it's not just a linguistic connection, although the word "inspire" does express this connectedness: Every time you consciously breathe in (*inspire*), you breathe *in spirit*, and the result is *inspiration*. I'm playing with words, but I'm also totally sincere. Whatever situation you are in, especially in a situation like loss, heartbreak or illness, spend a moment each day to breathe the conscious breath. It signals to your psyche, your body and your environment that you are choosing life, and soon you will see your reality responding to that choice and supporting the life-force energy within you. Deep, conscious breathing, by the way, is not just an excellent tool to calm and balance your nervous system, but it's also one of the fastest ways to relax your mind and find inner stability. In fact, breathing is the bridge between your physiology and your psyche. What does it take to tame the wild winds of change? Simply breathing them in, one breath at a time.

Fading Passion

Whether you feel it or not, your soul has a burning passion for living your human experiences. Perhaps you are going through a rough patch at the moment – just remember that your challenges don't have to dominate your life; your problems don't have to be your focus. What usually happens when we experience something difficult is that we try to analyse it, block out any uncomfortable feelings, judge what is happening as something "wrong that shouldn't be happening", and that is the moment when we tend to block our passion for life – we stop the energies from flowing. On a subconscious level, we think that by being less present with the difficult situation, *it* will become less present, but of course we are only sticking our head in the sand. Many of us feel a lack of passion in our lives simply because we have gotten stuck in the mind and have lost our ability to feel, sense and dream.

However, in addition to this very common occurrence there is another phenomenon that happens specifically as part of the self-realization process. What happens is that at some point you realize that you are a bit different from the norm – not better or worse, just different. You accept that you don't fit into the old roles and identities that other people gave you, so you release them. Now there is a void within you and an urgent desire to fill that emptiness with a new purpose. You may even enter a depression-like state. Your old passions fade away, but you don't know how to live without passion altogether, so you start to seek for a new passion. You cry out to your soul, to the universe: "What is my passion? Where is my passion? What am I supposed to be doing? What is my purpose, what is my next mission, goal, project? I feel worthless, doing nothing all day. Give me a reason to get up in the morning!"

So here you are, probably after countless lifetimes on Earth, moving from one external passion to another, but always having a passion: In some lifetimes it was a religious devotion, or a passion for family life, for artistic endeavours, spiritual growth, scientific advancement, philosophy, for serving your country, or perhaps protecting your tribe as a warrior. Whatever it was, you always had a role. Similarly, in the earlier years of this lifetime you've had passions. It could have been reading, musical expression, even spiritual passions such as meditating, energy healing, or social passions such as romantic relationships, being a parent and so on.

On a higher level, you have been orchestrating a trans-formation, and a lot of things that used to be significant to you begin to fade away. The fading away of your passion is not an accidental inconvenience; it happens for a purpose and it happens to every awakening human at some point in their journey. The reason for this is that your old passions have acted as glue, keeping you stuck in old patterns, in repetitive experiences. It's not that anyone or anything is stealing away your passion, it's simply that you arrive at a point of having completed so many human experiences that the old passions have served their purpose.

Another point to remember is that self-realization is an all-consuming metamorphosis. Truly, awakening is an all-or-nothing kind of business: either it affects all of your life, or it's not happening. Letting go of those familiar passions is actually an act of self-protection, because placing your passion both in the traditional human roles and in self-realization at the same time is like being simultaneously pulled into two different directions. I am by no means suggesting you to lose interest in your human life; what I'm saying is that the fading of passion is a natural part of the process of awakening, and its purpose is to create space in your life and within your perception of self for your free self, your "I am". In my experience, it's best not to fight against this phase, but instead allow it and understand its fleetingness. In practice, this means that when you arrive at the point where you simply feel no passion to live, yet you're not ready to die either, be okay with not having passion. I understand that it's much more fashionable to be ambitious and passionate, but allowing yourself to feel that inner void and emptiness is what eventually opens the door for the soul-passion to enter. It might be tempting at this stage to attend some workshop on motivation, but this would be like putting a bandage over the symptom – it can hide the wound for a while, but it actually prolongs the natural process.

Do not be discouraged, for the passion will eventually come back; passion is an integral part of your soul! But don't expect it to come back in the old way. When the passion comes back, it will be less focused on external things, such as activities or other humans. It will not belong to only one domain in your life, such as your career. It will not always be the fiery passion but it might come in as a cool, fresh breeze or a steady, warm glow. It will seep in through the cracks of your ego and pour into every molecule of your body and into every dimension of your life. At first, it might not be directed at anything external. It might be directed only at yourself, your sovereignty, your self-love and *being*ness. It won't make your ego exhilarated in the way that the old passion did; it will be more like a constant undercurrent of quiet joy. It will not always be exciting, or as pushy as you know passion to be. Whereas in the past your romantic relationships would inspire you to feel love, now it is self-love that will inspire you to feel passion for being in the company of another person. The new passion doesn't react very much to your external circumstances, but it is an independent presence that accompanies you, when you allow it.

This inner passion is not here to serve your mission; it's here to serve *you*. Most of us who are awakening are "old souls" and have spent many lifetimes here on Earth serving humanity. The idea of not focusing on serving others but instead focusing on the Self can be very daunting. We have come to feel comfortable in the role of service. There is nothing wrong with being in service, but there comes a time when being in service becomes an excuse for not looking at one's own issues. Obviously, I'm writing this book for conscious individuals, and for you my question is: What if you allowed life to serve you? Would it really be so bad to indulge yourself with your own attention and love? These are some of the questions that will rise to the surface as your old passions fade. Your inner soul-passion doesn't need to wait for you to be "worthy" of it because in your soul's eyes, there is no way that you could ever be unworthy. That's why I say: Give up the idea that you are here on some holy mission – perhaps you are, but the point is that your soul is passionate regardless of how holy or unholy the experiences of the human facet are. It's all right to do things just for the fun of it; you don't need to be so goddamn holy every minute of the day!

Having said all that, there are some practical things you can do to reconnect with your Soul-passion:

• Allow yourself to release the old expressions of passion. Letting go of the old dreams and old ambitions creates space for the new. Realize that your past self (including your past dreams) will never disappear, but will be transformed and integrated into the new you. In practice, this means allow yourself to mourn the death of past passions: Instead of suppressing the grief, stay with those feelings, and express them through journaling, for example.

• This one is especially for the women: Shift your focus from pleasing the world to pleasing yourself. When your life is filled up by too many have to's and should's, you are too distracted to enjoy life. One of the easiest ways to bring passion back into your reality is to shift your focus and purpose from getting things done to *receiving life*. This means enjoying the moment, enjoying yourself, and allowing yourself to view life as a gift that you and the universe are giving to yourself. For a day, pretend that your only purpose in life is to let it serve you, no matter what you are doing. When you go to work, notice how your work is supporting your wellbeing and joy. When something good happens to you, take it personally and receive it with pride. When you plan your dinner, ask yourself what do you feel like eating, what would bring you joy…

• One of the things that kills passion is being afraid of mistakes. "Mistakes" will happen, and that's okay; it's part of our humanity.

• Connect with your soul: Your soul is the unlimited source of your inner passion, and the more you connect with the soul in a conscious way, the more you will feel this inner source. There is no right or wrong way to connect with soul, but conscious breathing is one simple way. For example, you could close your eyes, take a few deep breaths and say: "Soul, I am ready to feel passion again. Show me how to feel my natural passion." Perhaps you don't feel something tangible right away, but keep your eyes open for the rest of the day and notice any changes.

- Breathe passion into a specific problem. Let's say, you just received an unpleasant email that triggered fear in you. Breathe the passion right into your body and into that fear – no thinking here, just do it. Allow passion to be part of every experience in your life, especially experiences that you don't usually connect with passion. It won't solve all your problems, but it will shift your perspective. Moments of financial struggles, relationship loss, emotional pain, or health problems are not the time to shut passion out – on the contrary, this is the time to invite passion to join your experience. Passion has a way of moving energy, and whenever there is a problem in your life, there is something within your energetic system that is not flowing freely.

- Shift your focus from thinking into feeling and sensing. For example, when reading a book, feel it with all your senses. Allow yourself to be a truly sensual being.

- One of the main problems with relationships (especially intimate relationships) is that we treat them as a source of passion. This is a common, but unfortunate misunderstanding; a relationship is the expression of passion, whereas your soul is the source of passion. You already *own* your passion and you don't need one specific person to awaken it. What you can do is take the burden off your relationship, and instead of viewing your relationship as the supplier of passion, view it as the place where you can share your passion with another being.

- Passion is natural. Don't force it. You can't will yourself into true passion, and you don't have to. If you make it into yet another goal that needs to be achieved, you've missed the point. You don't need to search for passion, because it is within you – instead, start *noticing* and *allowing* it. And please trust that it will come to you at the right time.

Loneliness – the Occupational Hazard of a Spiritual Pioneer

When you disconnect from our old life but have not yet landed in the new one, it's natural to feel lonely. You'll find yourself in the *in-between* zone, in the no-man's land. It is easy to feel lost or alone in this process, and in a way, it is appropriate because it will help you disconnect from your old energy sources. Solitude is essential in awakening; loneliness is not (though it's common). Loneliness is nothing more than a feeling of separation from your core Self reflected in the separation you feel from others. The anxiety related to loneliness stems from the fear of the void within, and the only reason you fear that void is because you are disconnected from it; once you reconnect with those fragmented parts of you, you will realize that the void isn't a scary black hole that will swallow you, but it's your depth. Integration, of course, is the solution to healing this separation and disconnection from your aspects and your core essence. The more you reconnect with all the parts of you, the more authentic and intimate your connections with other people will be. I will discuss the process of integration in depth in the next section of this book.

It is very important to take time to be with yourself, to really spend time being present with yourself and your feelings (without external stimulations such as TV or alcohol). In our society, we have lost the basic skill of being present with our feelings, and therefore have a tendency to distract ourselves whenever we feel something unpleasant. This has led to the current state of humanity, where many of us fear spending time alone in our own company. However, you will find that being in solitude is one of the most rejuvenating things you can do, especially if you are a sensitive person.

Something that is very helpful, in addition to spending time with yourself, is connecting with like-spirited humans. Find people, groups or places, both online and especially face-to-face, that resonate with you, with whom you can share your experiences of awakening. Don't be surprised if the people that you resonate with change after a while – it is really you who is changing.

If you are serious about enlightenment, then you definitely do not fit into the norms of society. Perhaps you've noticed this? Your interests might differ from those of your work colleagues, for example, and you might have difficulties to relating to your own family members. Most of us walking this path battle with the compromise of living within a society whilst staying in integrity with ourselves.

I have certainly felt anxiety because I was searching for a place and a profession where I would 'fit in'. This anxiety only lessened after I realized that it doesn't matter what I do as my human personality – what matters is how I do it. Instead of obsessing whether this job or that marriage fits in with your enlightenment, just choose enlightenment and see how your life flows and changes. Maybe the changes are external, but maybe not. If your relationship, for instance, is truly incompatible with your enlightenment experience, it will fall apart without any effort. If the relationship is still there, perhaps it serves your self-realization? Whether you're in a relationship or not, whether you have a job or not, can you accept that in some ways, you simply don't fit in?

I know from my experiences how painful it is to feel like an outsider and to feel disconnected from people with whom you once were close. This loneliness and false sense of separation can even lead to a deep depression, because we are a social species. The good thing is that we are living in an era where technology allows us to connect with like-minded people from all over the world in real-time. Chatting online is not the same as a physical hug from a friend, but what it does is show you that there are other people living on this planet who are facing the same issues as you.

As you integrate your relationship wounds, it will become a lot easier for you to attract people into your life that understand and respect you. Just because in the past awakening was traditionally a lonely path, it doesn't have to be that way in modern times. Your soul doesn't really need social connections to feel fulfilled, but your human aspect thrives on social interaction. And you happen to be both! Many people are going through their awakening right now, and although you will not resonate with all of them, there will be individuals or groups that you do resonate with. So keep looking for them if you haven't found "your crowd" yet, and always be attentive to your intuition – your gut will tell you whether a person or a group feels good to you or not.

Alchemizing Fear

Fear can be a catalyst for change, and in awakening, it is
a given. Of course, fear is part of every human's life, but
in awakening it is especially present because many of the
defence mechanisms used to cope with fear will disintegrate.
In awakening, we try to reconnect with our subconscious self,
which is where most of our fears reside. We have a biologically
and socially programmed instinct to reject and resist anything
that scares us. No matter how biological fear is, most of the
time it causes more harm than benefit. As psychologists have
claimed for the past century, supressing the fear doesn't
help either. Your job is to find that sweet spot where you
acknowledge your fear but you don't get stuck in it. The trick
is to let it wash through you. Let it strip off you everything
that is not real or not important anymore. And remember
that no matter how big your fear is, it plaes in comparison to
your consciousness and the love within you, because those are
unlimited.

Here are some practical steps you can take to alchemize fear:

1.   The first thing to do when we find ourselves in a state of
anxiety or fear is to consciously choose the 'safe space'. The safe
space is not a shield against dark energies or a white bubble
that you create around yourself – it's simply a choice that all
parts of you, in all dimensions, in all areas of your life are safe.
When you choose your safe space, you claim your sovereignty
and become aware of being the creator of your reality and
that in itself is empowering. Imagine that your inner self is a
house, and your fears are dark shadows. Instead of closing the
door to your fears and resisting them, creating a safe space

means opening the doors and the windows wide open, so that the light, warmth and fresh air flow in; you are not shielding yourself from the darkness, but the darkness will naturally either fade away or transform in the safe space. You create the safe space simply by taking a deep breath and choosing it. Make sure to be present and grounded in your body, though.

2.   Once you have chosen the safe space, allow yourself to feel the fear and all the other emotions that are present. That's right, don't try to get over your fear, don't push it away and don't run from it. Take a deep breath, and dive right into and through those feelings. This is called shadow work, and the principle behind it is that instead of pretending that those uncomfortable feelings aren't there, we allow ourselves to consciously sink into them, and by doing so we take the light of our awareness to illuminate those wounded or imbalanced parts of ourselves so that they can become lighter.

3.   While you are allowing those energies to flow through you (and remember, that's all they are – energies), imagine yourself observing your own emotions from a short distance. Realise that although the experience of fear is real, the fear is not who you are. You can allow fear to flow through you without holding onto it or identifying yourself with it. Like when you are standing in the rain without a cover and you get wet, you don't identify with the rain. You don't feel anxious about getting soaked, because you know it's a temporary state and it doesn't mean anything. It's just rain! What if we could take this approach with our emotions? Sure it's uncomfortable and inconvenient to get soaked by the energies of fear, but so what? It won't last forever, and it doesn't make you a less worthy person.

4.   If you can dis-identify yourself from the fear, keep breathing consciously and choose to integrate those aspects of fear. This is not an intellectual exercise, but a practice of divine surrender: Simply imagine and feel yourself handing those shadow parts of yourself over to your soul, trusting that she knows how to integrate, heal and transmute these parts.

5.   If it feels necessary or appropriate, you can now go back to the earthly situation that triggered the fear, and invite your divine consciousness to bring you a creative solution to resolve those energies. For example, if the anxiety was triggered by a conversation with your partner, you can invite your intuition to show you whether the issue needs addressing or not, and if yes, what would be the best approach. Often the creative solutions come to us when we are no longer in a state of fear, since fear is a great distraction from our intuition. The mind usually wants to jump straight to the task of finding solutions, but whenever we are in a state of fear, anxiety or panic, it's essential to *first* find our safe space. Otherwise our "solutions" will be based on fearful and skewed logic.

In addition, it's always a good idea to discern between a warning that comes from your intuition and a fear-instinct coming from your aspects and past experiences. Needless to say, most of the worry, anxiety, fear, nervousness and general feelings of unsafety are merely habitual reactions based on past experiences, but have nothing to do with the reality of your current moment. The body's nervous system is wired to protect us from danger by activating the sympathetic nervous system whenever we perceive danger or stress, and our body automatically reacts as if our survival was under threat. However, the truth is that our survival is rarely under real threat, meaning that most of the time it's a false alarm. This false alarm takes a considerable toll on our physical and mental health and wellbeing. Especially in the West, most of us have become adrenaline-junkies; in today's world, it's more common to be in a chronic state of stress than not. Again, just because it's normal, doesn't mean it's natural or healthy.

The question is: why are we so addicted to adrenaline? As with anything present in your life, fear serves you somehow – otherwise it wouldn't be there. One way in which fear has served the human aspect, is that fear makes it possible for us to play the game of duality and to experience contrast. Once we have experienced the contrast deeply and thoroughly, fear loses its value. It serves the human who wants to understand limitation and power, but it no longer serves the conscious master who is ready for ease and grace and trust. Ultimately it is up to you to choose whether to give into the distraction of fear, or whether to choose something new. Remember also that your fear is scarier than the objects of your fear, until you start to face it. The fear will get less overwhelming as you commit to releasing old patterns.

Treasures and Guardians

The dragon symbolizes the threshold of enlightenment. In my experience, it is useless to try to run, hide or fight these inner monsters, because they are there in your service. We tend to resist the dragons and demons that have been hidden for eons of time in our subconscious self. I would go so far as to claim that *what any human fears the most, is their own darkness.* Darkness, however, is nothing but a space within you that has not yet been touched by the light of your awareness and self-compassion. In the end, the only way to allow the alchemy is to surrender to it. But don't worry, your roots run deeper than you realize, keeping you anchored even in stormy weather.

These inner dragons that stand at the threshold of your enlightenment are not there to test your worthiness; they were placed there by your knowingness, to protect *you*, to make sure that you didn't cross over into embodied enlightenment before you were ready to handle the consequences. Sometimes consciousness is soft and subtle, like pink light that bathes you in love and peace. At other times, it's more like dynamite. Usually when consciousness is brought into this reality it's like a mirror that you can't escape and that shows you all of your thoughts, emotions, fears and desires – especially the ones that you'd rather not see. Most humans would sooner die than come face to face with their subconscious self, and that is not an exaggeration.[10]

It's no coincidence that two thousand years ago there were only a handful of conscious humans, and now there are millions of people who are beginning to awaken to their divinity – the time wasn't ready back then and now it is. Imagine that, instead of one Jesus, everyone had opened up to his or her consciousness 2,000 years ago. Wasn't there enough drama with one person publicly recognizing their divinity? Humanity wouldn't have been ready to face its own shadows two millennia ago, and

---

10 To gain a deeper understanding of this, I suggest reading *The Red Lion* by *Maria Szepes.*

you can't unveil your soul without also unveiling your wounds.
Even today, most of humanity is not ready for it, and we have
to respect everyone's chosen path – you can't force someone
to awaken any more than you can force someone to open his
heart.

Your essence is bulletproof and tougher than a diamond; your
soul cuts through illusion in a flash: The moment that darkness
enters the sphere of consciousness, it ceases to be dark.
However, your human body and mind are very fragile, and
need to be in a state of balance in order to handle the intensity
and purity of consciousness. The cells of your body cannot hold
such high frequencies unless you know how to move energies
effectively. Your mind needs time to adapt itself to this new,
transparent, and very simple clarity. This contrast between
the brightness of your soul and the frailty of the human is
almost comical in its extremity. Your inner monsters might be
troublesome and irritating, but they are making sure that you
are ready to channel something so clear and free into the sticky,
heavy density of 3-D reality. They will make sure that you can
go beyond your mind without losing your mind.

It is common for a person going through their awakening
to wish for the process to be quicker. There have been many
individuals who have tried to speed up their enlightenment,
tried to burst through at breakneck speed. And most of
them ended up on the other side of the veil sooner than
intended, because their body couldn't handle the intensity
of the transformation. Or they lost their mind in the process.
Complete self-actualization is an intense process no matter
what, but rushing through it can really backfire.

Whenever you feel overwhelmed by your dragons and demons, be very gentle and compassionate with yourself, and consistently return to the trust that everything truly is okay, even if you can't see it right now. Your human self is just going through some wild experiences, and no matter what happens, the essence of you is in a state of perfect peace and balance. Your eternal essence can never be damaged, stolen, wounded, lost or separated; it exists, *no matter what*. When life seems treacherous and you are afraid of your own darkness, remember the treasure that it's guarding.

Whilst awakening is not a treasure hunt, you will uncover some truly magical gems in the process. The diamond serves as a beautiful metaphor for the alchemical transformation of the Self: Underneath Earth's surface, diamonds are forged under intense heat and pressure. When they finally rise to the surface, they are the hardest natural substance found on the planet, yet they radiate undeniable beauty and clarity. In your spiritual awakening, you will experience intense pressure that will transform you deep within and burn everything that was not clear. Know that each challenge that you face, polishes your clarity and that you will emerge from the "underground" of your own subconscious with an irrefutable, multi-faceted, and transparent brilliance. You'll know that you are ready for those treasures when you are no longer afraid of your own underground.

It's All About Integration

Home, Sweet Home

~ Integration is synchronizing your past, present and future into one point of presence called I am here. ~

Somewhere in the midst of all the chaos, you enter the next stage of awakening, where the reconnection of all your parts takes place. You thought it was about piecing your life back together, but it's really about piecing all of you together. It's so very human to see the small picture: your human personality is doing whatever it can to heal, improve, save, protect or embellish the life of the human without being aware of the context or realizing what is really happening. It's as if the human was so busy rearranging the furniture that it doesn't notice how the plumbing is being redone, how the walls are in the process of being ripped down and the electricity is being rewired. And now the human is all covered up in dust and frustrated, because it doesn't understand why the walls shake, why the lights keep flickering and why it's so noisy. When you enter this phase of your awakening, it's not enough to decorate your life a bit or to apply cosmetic changes to your human identity; integration is about going to the core of you. You are literally, chemically, rewiring yourself. When we reconstruct a house, we accept all the mess, because we know that it's temporary and we understand its necessity – what if you could apply that level of nonchalance to your inner reconstruction?

You'll know that you're entering this phase of your awakening, when you start to become conscious of your shadow-self – the

111

basement within the house of the 'I am'.

The moment you consciously choose enlightenment, you also choose integration: The integration of your soul *and* all the scattered aspects of all your human lifetimes into one whole, embodied, multiplicity consciousness. Integration means welcoming all the lost, fractured and polarized parts back home to your core, until one day you realize that you're not just white or black, but you are all the shades of the spectrum, just like everyone else, too. Other words for integration are shadow work, or healing. It is healing at the deepest level, as opposed to relieving, suppressing or eliminating the symptoms. Integration is the most natural and effective way to heal on all levels: Physical, emotional and mental. Unlike the methods of processing that are common in some approaches of psychotherapy, integration is not at all intellectual. Anybody who is healing himself at the deepest levels – whether his wounds are physical or emotional – is doing integration, even if he is not on a so-called spiritual path. In awakening, however, integration is inevitable. In addition to integrating your wounded aspects, in awakening specifically, you also integrate your divinity. Thus, it can be said that integration is truly the doorway to enlightenment.

Your shadow aspects are not some random ghosts haunting you, although it may feel that way because much like ghosts, your past will be catching up with you. Your past will come into your dreams at night, and flood into your memories during the day, until you give it some attention. When this happens, know that your past is only knocking on your door because it wants to be integrated. You don't need to go digging for your past, because that will mess with the natural process of integration (and make your life more difficult) – just don't ignore it when it naturally rises to the surface. Your current incarnation then becomes the anchor, the Holy Grail, and the home of all your experiences and facets. In other words, your 'body of consciousness', that composite of your body, mind and spirit, becomes the vessel in which the alchemy of integration takes place. Awakening is not about you, the human ego, returning home to your divinity, but rather it is about your divinity returning to your embodied awareness. You are the *ascendee* (a term coined by master Tobias), creating a new home of your soul, in the here and now.

~ Your true Self isn't higher, it's underground. ~

When you choose to be present in the now moment, present in the body that anchors your spirit, you can receive all that you are into one point of presence. You reconnect with your inner dimensions. Integration is like channelling all your past lives and future potentials into this moment, and distilling all aspects of yourself into a whole *oneness* of Self. You will still be a multi-dimensional being, but now the different dimensions of 'you' begin to be aware of each other. 'You' become a plural, meaning that you become aware of existing in many realities simultaneously, yet centred in the 'here and now' of the physical dimension. This oneness of you is connected with the oneness of All That Is, with the consciousness pulsing through every atom in the universe and beyond, yet you are also sovereign through the realization of freedom. Sovereignty of the divine self and oneness of all consciousness are not contradictions, except when we try to understand these concepts through the filters of the limited mind.

In the puzzle-analogy, this is the phase when the puzzle pieces fall into place. However, it is not your mind, but your soul, that collects the scattered pieces and places them into a new order. You can't see the full picture yet, but you can trust that if you keep putting the fragmented pieces together, one day a beautiful picture will emerge and it will all make sense. Ultimately, integration cannot be done through mental processing, because most of these 'puzzle pieces' (also called soul fragments or aspects in spiritual literature) are stuck in our *subconscious* self. Sometimes the only thing you can hold onto is trust. Still, every now and then, you'll feel that inner 'click', like a puzzle piece snapping into place, and it feels so good, because you know that you've just integrated an aspect that was haunting you for ages. Integration may be tough at times, but it's not complicated. To put it simply, it's about tying up loose ends, letting go of old karma and freeing energy that has been stuck for lifetimes. This is the phase in your spiritual journey, when all the battles have been fought, and now it's just about cleaning up the mess and accepting that there is nothing more to battle.

Aspectology: A Spiritual Psychology[11]

"Honey it wasn't me, it was my aspect..." said the aspect.

In order to allow integration to take place, we must understand

---

11 'Aspectology' is the name of the school created by Tobias of the Crimson Council, and is a new energy-approach to psychology: www. crimsoncircle.com/Events/Advanced-Studies/Advanced-Studies-Classes/Aspectology. Similar ideas can also be found in Gestalt psychotherapy.

what aspects are and how to deal with them. Aspects are not your true identity, but temporary identities rather like costumes that you (as the soul) wear so that you can experience life on Earth. Aspects are the specific perspectives that your soul creates to experience the contrast of light and dark; your various lifetimes are playful experiments created by the soul to explore all the shades of the rainbow.

Aspects are the often over-looked key to human psychology. We wear our human identities like masks, and we are always playing roles. Your profession, your position in the family, and your personality are examples of roles that you are playing. What we call 'personality' is really just a compilation of the aspects within us that are most dominant or most visible. Another word for this collection of aspects is 'the ego' as used by many spiritual teachers. Although the ego has a bad reputation, aspects only become problematic when we are unaware of them and their games. This doesn't mean that your personality and your roles are a lie, or pretence, but they are temporary expressions of your eternal Self. They are creations of the core consciousness that you truly are. If you were to paint a painting, it would be an expression of you, but you would know that the painting is not really you. Similarly, your human identity is merely an expression of your creator Self. Often, we don't acknowledge the fleetingness of our human personality, because the human has learnt to identify with her roles, rather than with her soul.

In addition to roles and identities, aspects come in many other forms, like our emotions. For example, anytime you get triggered by something, it's an un-integrated aspect of yours coming to the surface. It's calling for your attention and letting you know that it still has an unmet need. These shadow aspects are often called 'inner children' in spiritual literature, because most of our wounded aspects were born out of childhood experiences. Archetypes are another group of aspects, as are the id, the ego and the superego described by Freud. We all have countless aspects, some that are integrated and whole, others that are wounded and fragmented from the Self. Of course, these aspects are never actually separated from the true self; what causes suffering is when an aspect *perceives* and believes itself to be separated from the whole.

Portrait of a Wounded Aspect

Having aspects is part of being human, but the problem arises when an aspect gets seemingly fractured and separated from the wholeness of you. Whenever you as the human experiences a traumatic or life-threatening situation (or a situation that is emotionally threatening, such as a child not knowing where his or her mother is), the survival instinct kicks in and takes over: the human goes into a state of shock, and unconsciously creates an aspect that will carry the wound for her, because the trauma is simply too much for the human to deal with in that moment of threat. This happens because the human is physiologically conditioned into prioritizing survival over emotional wellbeing: If the priority were emotional wellbeing, we would not have the ability to suppress painful emotions for the sake of survival, but would instead direct our efforts at regaining emotional balance. The usual reality, however, is that in the event of trauma or danger, we unconsciously, and due to chemicals such as adrenaline, supress the emotional pain. This suppressed emotion is what we call an aspect.

This aspect then separates from the human personality, so that she doesn't have to identify with the trauma and can go on with her life. It makes survival easier in the short run. The aspect, however, remains stuck in the past, and in a way, remains ostracized from the rest of the self. This means that until the aspect is integrated again, part of the person's stream of consciousness will remain stuck with it. It is as if the rest of her consciousness moved forward into the future with her, but a ray of it remained stuck to the past. These wounded aspects are indeed like ghosts, walled into a frozen time-loop by the pain of unresolved trauma. To simplify, shadow aspects are manifestations of traumatic experiences. This is how grey or dark aspects are created. Although these aspects feel very separate from your "normal identity", they always remain hooked or connected to the present you, which is how they continue to feed on your energy and influence your choices. On an electro-magnetic level, a part of your energy is constantly leaking into these aspects, until you consciously integrate them. Energetically traumas appear as cuts or holes in your aura, each hole being like a vortex into the memory of the event that created the aspect.

What causes trauma is not pain in and of itself; what causes trauma is when the pain (be it physical or emotional) is not being acknowledged and resolved. These stuck energies then show up from time to time, whenever triggered, as emotional, mental or physical reactions or patterns. Perhaps you then develop an addiction or a physical imbalance, without being aware of its origin in a possibly forgotten childhood experience. These wounded aspects are in fact the cause of any disease and any self-harming habits. Although trauma can be experienced at any point in life, usually the traumatic events taking place in adolescence or adulthood are repetitions of early-childhood trauma. A traumatic experience in this context is any experience that is shocking or overwhelming to the individual. It could be caused by one dramatic experience, or many small experiences such as emotional neglect.

When a traumatic experience remains unresolved, the individual sometimes unconsciously recreates a similar emotional experience to the original one, in an attempt to find resolution. This is often the case, even though on a surface level, the experiences of the adult might seem to have very little in common with the experiences of an infant. Post-Traumatic Stress Disorder as well as Personality Disorders are examples of the more explicit manifestations of dark aspects. If you look at a person with Dissociative Identity Disorder (what used to be called Multiple Personality Disorder), you can see a blatant example of aspects that are very fragmented from the conscious self. From my perspective, all of us experience this condition, although most of us to a much lesser extent.

The darker the aspect, the more separated its identity is from your soul, yet even the darkest aspect always contains a spark of the original divinity that created it. Always remember that your aspects are manifestations of your experiences, but they are not the totality of who you are. They will make you feel small, confused, lonely and separated (because that's the way they feel), but even these feelings are not the limitless consciousness at the core of your being. A separated aspect will tell you stories about who you are and what you should identify with. Even these thoughts and stories are aspects, tiny drops of an infinite ocean that is your core Self.

Referring to the earlier analogy, we are such talented actors that we forgot that we are just acting. We have forgotten that we are God playing a limited human, because we have created a very convincing stage with very real props. (Often the soul that incarnates as a human intentionally chooses to forget its divine identity, so that it can focus on the experience of being human. It is this illusion that allows us to experience contrast.) It is common to feel stuck in a particular role in life, but in fact, no role can limit you unless you play along with that belief. The moment you realize your true creator-nature, you also realize how transient your roles are. For example, if you were born into poverty, it's easy to get stuck with that role of being poor and to believe that poverty is your future as well. However, your destiny is never to stay stuck in a role you dislike, unless you choose that experience. The permanence or density of reality is one of the illusions that we are awakening from.

Every time the human has a new experience, a new aspect is created. With every new aspect, the soul gathers wisdom. There comes a point in the journey of the soul when it feels that it has collected enough wisdom from its experiences on Earth, when it has experienced enough polarity and contrast to know all that it is not, and therefore is ready to experience all *that it is*. There comes a point when the human decides it is ready to complete its cycles of being human, when it is ready to remember who it really is, and therefore ready to realize its connection to soul. This is the point when it's time to return all those aspects home and to awaken to the remembrance of the identity behind the identities. Indeed, enlightenment is all about returning these run-away aspects to the love of your soul.

This process starts by becoming conscious of the roles that you are playing: When you start to play those roles consciously rather than automatically identifying with them, your *consciousness becomes an active participant in your human life* rather than merely a passive spectator. When you awaken, you realize that you don't have to take your human roles so seriously anymore, and that you can even have fun with them.

Conscious Integration

~ Beauty is integrated contrast. ~

Imagine that someone was mean to you when you were five years old, and now you still have an unconscious pattern of low self-esteem – because of a single sentence spoken to you decades ago! It happens. Perhaps you think you have high self-esteem, but you're not conscious of this aspect that is still stuck in the past and unbeknownst to you influencing which experiences you attract into your life. You simply end up making self-sabotaging choices in your life. Of course, it's not the grown-up, intelligent version of you who is making these self-harming choices, but it is a wounded aspect that is acting through you – or rather, behind your back, so to speak, in an attempt to get its needs met. The question is, how can these wounded aspects be integrated?

You, as the human, do not need to *do* anything except be very present in your body, in the 'here and now', observing and allowing the process. You don't need a strategy for integration; you simply integrate an aspect whenever you become aware of one, usually by being triggered. At the end of this Part of the book, you'll find a step-by-step guide for integrating aspects when you feel triggered by something. For now, here's a brief overview of the process. The integration itself happens through *your conscious choice*, through *allowing* and *observing*: Observe any emotions and thoughts that come up (these are manifestations of the aspects). This means not running away from unpleasant feelings, but instead opening the door wide open to whatever you are feeling, in the understanding that the aspects are here to return to the unity of you. Allowing the process means trusting that your soul knows how to integrate even the darkest of your "monsters", and your soul does it without a trace of judgement, guilt or shame. Be aware, not afraid. When you feel like a haunted house, don't be afraid of your aspects. They like to feed on your fear, but remember that they are just expressions of your past experiences. Most of the ghosts we are afraid of are our own aspects, by the way. We all have grey and dark aspects, so you don't need to worry about being too special. This is not to say that you should ignore or push away your fear. Again, open the door to your soul and allow the fear to just be – and sooner or later it will naturally return to its neutral state. Your soul is the one who does all the work, so do not try to mentally control or steer the integration process. Your job, as the human, is to stay very still and balanced and present. To use a metaphor, your aspects are like the wind and the rain and the sunshine, and this is the time for you to be the tree: to stay grounded, centred and deeply rooted in your truth.

With each aspect that is integrated, the light of your awareness shines brighter, and you realize that although you have experienced the darkest of the dark and the lightest of the light, your eternal essence always has been and always will be clear and unaffected by the experiences of the human. There is no aspect that your soul cannot integrate, and no shadow dark enough that your soul's light cannot illuminate it. It's like being in the darkest of rooms, but once you open the curtains and let the rays of sunlight flow into the room, darkness cannot remain dark. Remember also, that it is often beneath the darkest shadows that the shiniest treasures can be found. In awakening, you will also integrate long-lost aspects of beauty, strength and talent, but it is often beneath the darkness where these are found. Never go looking for the shiny aspects, unless you are prepared to face your shadows first.

Are you playing your roles, or are your roles playing you?

Most people literally live their entire life through their aspects, instead of allowing their true essence to fill their body, mind and life. Their aspects are acting through them to interact with the aspects of other people. Like a marionette that is controlled by the puppet master, most people are rarely conscious of being played by their aspects. They believe they are victims of their fate, of other people, or of outside circumstances, but really, they are just victims of their own aspects. This is the main difference between someone who is 'awake' and someone who is not yet awakening. It is quite easy to remain unconscious of your dark aspects, because they dwell deep within your subconscious mind, and because they are very dis-identified from you. Although the aspect feels separated from you, it will try to act through you, so that you will think that a certain emotion is your emotion. These dark aspects are always trying to play power games through you and react to other people's power games. In a way, this whole playing field of Earth was created so that we learn about energies and about contrast, and in that context aspects have been useful. There comes a time, however, when both the soul and the human decide they have learned enough and gained enough experiences, and that is the time for the aspects to lay down their positions and to retire, in a manner of speaking.

Eckhart Tolle is one of the modern masters teaching presence. Being present is crucial if you choose mastery. By 'mastery' I mean living consciously and being in charge of your life, rather than letting your subconscious self call the shots. Mastery has nothing to do with other people, and it isn't about controlling the weather, your surroundings or even your feelings. Those are magician's tricks – fun, but quite irrelevant in the grand scheme of things. What is relevant, though, is being the master of your own life. True mastery is being so present that you are not unconsciously letting your aspects act through you; it's when every action you take (or don't take) is a conscious, chosen response, rather than an automatic unwanted reaction. You can only be the master of your life if you are very present; otherwise your aspects will fill the vacancy. Every time you breathe consciously, you become more present. Through breathing, the essence of you fills your body, and only then will it be possible to act from an authentic, clear and true place rather than a conditioned, fear-driven place. Mastery may roll off the tongue easily, but of course it takes extensive changes in your life and psyche to realize it. It also takes patience. Yet it is important to know that with time, mastery *is* a possibility and a reality for anyone who is truly committed to their self-realization.

When we start to become aware of our darker aspects, it is

easy to slip into shame, guilt and self-judgement, because we suddenly see how unconscious we have been all our lives. When our masks are stripped off, all our chaotic, "dark" aspects that we previously weren't even aware of, are spilling into our lives. We have the unhealthy habit of judging ourselves and because of that, also judging others. Imagine what you would do all day if you didn't judge yourself or others – or think about their judgements? It is worthwhile trying it out. For example, whenever you approve of someone, it means you have first judged whether that person is worthy of your approval. Feeling shame, guilt and judgement are examples of your shadow aspects acting through you. Whenever these feelings show up, embrace the opportunity to integrate them. And remember that unlike in the Greek myth of Pandora, this treasure chest of awakening is not only filled with shadows, but also with the hidden gems of your soul.

Do not fall into the trap of thinking that you have to control your aspects. You can't control them, because the really tricky ones are far too subconscious for you to control them through mental intention. The thing to do with aspects is to be aware of them, to observe them, to stay present with them and most importantly, to *not let them distract you* from your inner balance. When you continue to breathe calmly and insist on focusing on your balance no matter what tumultuous emotions are showing up, then your aspects will naturally integrate sooner or later. It is the art of being in the state of 'and': Allowing yourself to really feel the uncomfortable feelings, opening up to all parts of you *and*, at the same time, focusing on your balance. When you keep your focus on your inner balance instead of fighting with the aspects, you create a safe haven, and the aspects will eventually feel safe enough to drop their guard and let go of their "rebellion". Keeping your focus on your self-love and choosing to stay calm without avoiding the emotions is the key to integration.

Non-reaction as a Short Cut to Mastery

Non-reaction is one of the key elements of aspect-integration. As you will quickly notice, it has nothing to do with being passive. Not reacting to your own aspects or to the aspects of other people will at first be incredibly difficult, but soon enough you will feel the great freedom and ease that it brings into your life. Non-reaction means that you do not automatically react to a surge of emotion, but instead you observe the emotion and stay present with it, and then consciously choose how you respond to the situation. There is a moment between your button being pushed, and your reaction to that event, and this is the moment when you can become conscious of what is happening. You can press the 'pause' button and take a deep breath. You can notice that it's your button that is being pushed, you can take responsibility for that emotion, and you can breathe with the emotion until it has washed through you. It is about choosing responsibility versus choosing blame, and realizing that when you choose responsibility you are much stronger than when you slip into the victim role of blaming someone or something.

Your choice of taking responsibility has nothing to do with anybody else in the situation; it's just about you and your mastery. Are you more committed to mastery, or to being right? Non-reaction doesn't mean that you ignore or push down your emotions; it means that you observe them, with compassion for yourself, and at the same time, you dis-identify yourself from them. It means that no matter how intense an emotion may be, you perceive it as your experience rather than as your identity. Your past doesn't make you a victim in this moment unless you choose to play the victim role. There are many roles that we can get trapped in; the reason why I specifically talk about the victim role is that this is one of the most common and limiting roles that we play – especially those of us who are awakening.

When you use your free will to take responsibility of your creations, you empower yourself – you give yourself freedom. Emotions are just energy passing through you, so let that energy pass through without resistance! Do what you need to do, in order not let your aspects act through you: Perhaps you need to be alone for a few minutes, and punch a pillow or shake the frustration loose. A useful tip is to try to stay as present as possible when you express strong emotions. When you are truly present, the expression of emotions to other people doesn't cause damage. Also consider that the emotion doesn't need to be seen by others as much as it needs to be seen by you; when you express emotions, do it first for yourself, in a space of self-compassion. Experiment with new ways of responding to emotional triggers. Non-reaction is like meditation in action – once you get the hang of it, it's easy (it's just the first thousand times that trip you up).

Clarity vs. Control

Commitment to your expansion and self-love is essential, however, you can be committed without the need of control. On this path, force is an obsolete technique. Eventually any technique to embody your consciousness is an obsolete technique, because working your way through awakening simply doesn't work. In so many ways, awakening is an act of divine surrender. What works for me is to be clear instead of controlling, and to be consciously relaxed rather than unconsciously stressed. Sure, it's hard to let go of the battles, but only because we are not used to doing things the easy way.

When the time comes and things seem chaotic, confusing, uncontrollable, overwhelming, or intense – take a deep breath. This is the moment to be very present in your body, and to know (have clarity) that this is what you have chosen. Now is the time to remember that this is your awakening in the unfolding, and everything is as it should be. It is just your ego being peeled away layer by layer, so that the raw, true, crystalline You can shine brighter. This is the time to breathe with joy, breathe with sadness, and breathe with whatever is… Open your eyes in the darkness and you will see the light shining from within you. Enlightenment doesn't require *any* type of control; it just requires your trust and commitment to your own ever-expanding truth, rather than the limited beliefs of the aspects.

Pitfalls of Ascension

~ Transformation is a spiral dance, not a clean cut. ~

They say that the biggest distractions to enlightenment come at the eve of your realization. Why? Because that's when you are ready to face them. Let yourself dance into your new self one spiral twist at a time, and don't expect it to be done in one take.

There are two main approaches to the spiritual path: The first one is focusing on the light, on anything that makes you feel better – the theory being that by feeling good, you place yourself in a higher vibration that attracts more good things into your life so that eventually your whole reality, everything that surrounds you or comes into contact with you, mirrors this light. This approach explains all the emphasis that is placed by the New Age community on the 'law of attraction'. My experience is that this approach doesn't work by itself, because it only addresses one side of the self – the light.

Another approach to the spiritual path is to dive straight into your shadows. This approach is symbolized by the myth of Persephone, the Greek deity who descends into the underworld and her own subconscious. Much of traditional psychology (the psychodynamic school of psychology) is also based on the idea that the root of our current problems lies in the hidden and forgotten aspects of our consciousness. The idea here is that if we consciously explore our shadow aspects, we bring awareness into places that have been covered by unawareness, and thus the dark transforms into light (awareness).

We don't start our awakening journey by consciously choosing which approach to take, but most of us naturally steer towards one of these two directions. It is not uncommon for the spiritual seeker to swing from one extreme to the other, until these experiences intertwine in a natural flow that incorporates both approaches. There is no need to mentally direct your path, since the whole process is natural.

Both approaches have their pitfalls, and can be used as spiritual bypass techniques, meaning that they can be used as methods to avoid facing our true self. The problem with focusing only on the light is that you easily end up 'fixing' your life and your current feeling-state on a cosmetic level, but you continue carrying unhealed wounds on a deeper level. What happens as a result is that those dark (wounded) aspects of you that you are not even aware of, attract situations into your life that are correspondingly dark. And then you wonder how it is possible that after all your efforts of being a 'light-worker', you are still caught in low frequency vibrations. The fact is that your resistance towards the dark is what will attract it to you. This is not some twisted metaphysical karma; it happens because on a soul-level we all long to be whole, and that means returning the dark fragments back to the core of us.

The pitfall of focusing only on your shadows is that you can momentarily get lost in your own desperation, and lose the wider perspective. If you feel all your dark aspects, it is easy to forget that you are divine, and so much bigger than those fleeting shadows. No matter how strong or powerful those dark aspects seem, they are like a raindrop to the ocean of your soul. The trick is to remember that when a shadow aspect surprises you.

The Alchemy of Light and Darkness

~ Everything beautiful can be twisted, but anything tainted can be transformed into something beautiful. ~

Ultimately both paths lead to the same point: the marriage of light and dark. True metaphysical alchemy isn't about turning black into white; what happens in the merging of light and darkness is that a third reality, a new perspective emerges – a reality in which light and darkness can co-exist in harmony, without having the charge, the tension or the polarization that they previously had. They are allowed and accepted to such an extent that they are no longer opposites, but rather two qualities that dance with each other, coming together and falling apart naturally, always expanding. As they dance together, they birth a new quality, which is clear energy. In other words, light and dark become neutral; they no longer carry the weight of "good" and "bad" attached to them. Darkness might exist in the form of feelings, such as a surge of sadness or anger, but it is no longer perceived as evil or as something that "shouldn't be what it is". Integrated darkness is no longer demonized or placed in opposition to light.

What causes pain is never darkness itself, but the separation from it. Pain is caused by our separation from our own aspects. Pain is a part within our psyche calling for our attention. Separation is the deepest illusion in this universe, and therefore it causes the deepest emotional pain. However, once we allow ourselves to reconnect with our own darkness (in other words, acknowledge it, be present with it and accept it *as it is*), all the pain is released from that aspect or experience. It doesn't mean that this darkness then becomes light, but it becomes beautiful and meaningful – darkness becomes the shadow that gives your light its depth, and makes your light shine with even more brightness. Your darkness becomes the dark blue sky that brings out the radiance of the stars. At the moment of integration, you realize that all of us have elements of light and dark within us, and that darkness is something natural. You realize that darkness isn't evil, and that it can exist peacefully unattached to shame or guilt.

Un-integrated shadow aspects can lead us to act in an abusive manner if they are neglected, supressed, or fragmented, because they need to come out somehow. Energy can never remain stuck forever; it always seeks resolution. If we try to condense stuck energy within us or lock it up, it can and will blow things up. If we allow the aspects to return to us by owning them, without letting them take over our behaviour, but simply by allowing ourselves to feel them, observe them and be aware of them, they will naturally transform into a balanced version of themselves. The inner master doesn't try to transfigure anger into peace or sadness into joy; the master expands his or her perspective of the anger or the sadness from something that is unwanted to something that is seen and accepted, which gives the emotion the space to expand and shift naturally – without manipulation or force. When this happens, the aspect returns into a kind of neutral state: Its wisdom returns to soul, but its pain is released.

Experiential Metaphysics: How to Integrate Aspects

1.   The first step of integration is to become aware of an aspect that is trying to act through you. Usually an un-integrated aspect shows up in the form of an emotional or mental reaction: For example, someone says something to you and suddenly you feel a surge of anger, and you feel an immediate urge to react (the emotion itself is an automatic reaction that indicates the presence of an aspect). Feeling shame, guilt, fear, powerlessness, emotional exhaustion, depression, confusion or numbness are all definite signs of an aspect. Feeling judgement either towards yourself or someone else is another typical example of an aspect acting through you.

2.　Perhaps the most important thing you can do for integration is to create a safe space. Dark aspects were created in the first place because of a situation where you didn't feel safe or loved. In childhood, feeling loved is synonymous with feeling safe. Like run-away children, these aspects will return when they feel it's safe (in other words, when you feel safe). Create a safe space by making a conscious choice to be in a safe space, and by being present in your body. Remember that your essence is always safe, no matter what happens to your human expression. On a practical level, make sure that you feel safe in your home, in your body, in your life and your relationships. Daily conscious breathing (inhaling through the nose and slowly exhaling through the nose or the mouth) is one of the best ways to create a safe space. If you don't know where to start because the fear is so overwhelming, start with simple physical actions: take a warm bath, make yourself a cup of tea, clean your bedroom etc. Comfortable physical conditions are not necessary for us to feel safe, but they sure help a lot.

3.　The moment you feel triggered by something, observe the aspect/emotion/belief and breathe with it, allowing your consciousness and your breath to flow through the aspect. Do not identify with it, and do not let the emotion act through you.

You might be tempted to try to change or control your aspects, but it would be wiser to not interact with them in any way other than being present with them. That's when the transformation happens naturally. The moment you start negotiating or trying to change your dark aspects, you will get confused, because these aspects are very hurt and therefore can be very hurtful. The aspects will try to seduce you to fight and react, but if you consistently choose not to fight, not even to defend yourself but instead stay centred in your safe space of presence and non-judgment, then integration follows automatically.

4. Acknowledge that this aspect has served you in the past, and then make a clear choice to release it from its role. You don't need to do anything other than be clear about your choice, and continue breathing deeply and consciously to keep the energies flowing. All healing and integration happens by allowing stuck energies to flow again. You don't need to be able to feel or sense energies; you'll know that the energies are starting to flow when feelings like heaviness, numbness, frozenness, resistance, intensity, anger, compression or stickiness begin to lift, and when you start to feel lighter, more open, more expansive or more relaxed. You'll know that the aspect has been integrated when you feel a sense of relief, or when you experience a shift in your breathing: when you feel the breath reaching deeper, becoming lighter or flowing with greater ease.

5. To re-cap: When you get triggered, try not to react in any way (externally or internally), but instead observe your emotions and body sensations, and breathe deeply. Choose a safe space and be very present in the here and now, in your body. Make a clear choice to release the aspect from its role, inviting it to return to the oneness of Self. Do not fear or fight the aspect, do not try to change it. Breathe and keep the energies moving until you feel a sense of relief, completion or lightness.

How do you know when an aspect is integrated for good? The moment you integrate an old pattern or identity fully, the new will enter. If the new hasn't entered your life yet, it means a part of you is still holding onto the past.

If some part or other of your ego doesn't break at least once a week on your path from awakening into mastery, you are holding back regarding inner transformation. That may sound harsh, but after having experienced the death of your ego a thousand times, you'll realize that the end of your ego is not the end of You. You will also realize that the ego doesn't vanish into thin air just because you are becoming conscious. What changes is that whilst the ego continues to follow you like a shadow, it no longer dominates your life – and that's something to be proud of! Integration will never become comfortable, so don't wait for that, but it will become bearable and much quicker. Like a professional athlete who might never become comfortable with competition, but learns how to work with it, you will learn to work with integration rather than against it. Whether we call it healing, self-growth or spiritual enlightenment, it's really all about integration. And in case you are wondering, integrating the parts of you that are suffering is not an endless quest. Expansion might be a never-ending adventure, but suffering is one of those things that we absolutely can move beyond. Enlightenment is when you give yourself total permission to accept all your experiences, without exceptions, and allow yourself to expand beyond them. Nobody else can give you the permission of self-acceptance and enlightenment but you.

The Soul Surrender

~ They talk about ascension, but it's really about falling! ~

Enlightenment is non-linear. That means that the last phase of the realization of your enlightenment isn't just a linear progression of the earlier phases of your awakening, but more like a circle that is closing; it is a point of *convergence*. It's the merging of the parts of you that remember who you are with the parts of you that were in a state of spiritual amnesia. This is the part when all the concepts will fail you, because it is time to go beyond concepts. This stage is all about relaxing, letting go of struggle and surrendering to your true, divine embodied self.

As mentioned before, one cannot achieve enlightenment through any forced discipline. If you can't help being disciplined, be disciplined about receiving enlightenment and about releasing effort. That is challenging enough, for it goes against our conditioning of what a good or successful person is! Discipline and tenacity might have catalysed your awakening and brought you to this point, however, forceful techniques, or any techniques for that matter, will never carry you across the threshold of your enlightenment. Any method that restricts or suppresses your natural self will be de-lightening rather than enlightening – and so far I haven't come across any method that doesn't feel restrictive sooner or later, except for the "methods" of being present and breathing consciously. Here you have come to a point where no quantity or quality of methods, techniques or systems will bring you further. You simply cannot force, think, try, practice or strategize your way across the final threshold. If you could, there would be a lot more ascended masters than there are (around 9700 according to the angelic gossip I've heard).

If there is no procedure to follow, no technique to master, then how does one do it? First of all, the soul is already fully realized. Your responsibility as the human is to allow the transformation in this *present moment*, and to allow the layers of human personality to loosen up like the petals of a blooming flower to reveal the authentic self to emerge from within you. It's not about trying – as a matter of fact, it's best to let go of trying altogether: Of trying to be more perfect, more intelligent, more conscious, more anything. Just enjoy being whatever and whoever you are right now. The whole concept of growing, learning, searching and improving yourself works in the early stages of awakening, but once you come to a specific point (a point where you feel very comfortable with self-improvement), it's time to let go of that goal as well. Try no more, or try softer if you must try.

In this phase there is nothing left but mastery and the distractions that make you forget about your mastery. It is often in the last moments before realization that the greatest distractions come your way. If you feel like you are going backwards rather than moving closer to realization, you are not. You cannot go backwards, but you can get temporarily lost in the distractions. You don't really go forward either, because from a non-linear perspective, you are already enlightened. You are in the process of allowing your human self to remember and accept your already enlightened, true nature.

Because the mind is what it is, it might still try to play its usual tricks, despite your highly evolved consciousness; interfering thoughts and emotions will continue to come and go. You don't need to control the mind – instead, you can be aware of it and identify with your consciousness rather than with your thoughts and emotions. You can sink into the still space and depth between the noisy thoughts. Your mind will continuously tell you that you need to keep learning, planning and controlling your enlightenment. What I have found helpful is to involve the mind in my spiritual journey in a way that is supportive to my experience – I give my mind a task to distract it: The directive to *observe* what is happening around me and within me. Simply being present and observing the flow of life creates space between what is happening to me and who I am. Relaxed presence will calm the mind. Enlightenment is non-conceptual and can literally drive the mind crazy; it's helpful to give the mind a concrete task that it can comprehend, but that doesn't interfere with the allowing of your realization.

Top 10 Distractions on the Way to Enlightenment

Below is a list of the most common obstacles that distract us from crossing over the threshold into embodied enlightenment. If these apply to you, ask yourself: why do you hold onto that challenge?

1.   **Drama**: Most humans are unconsciously addicted to drama, suffering and the neurochemicals that are released in stressful situations. In other words, we are conditioned into feeling that drama is something normal. In awakening, we start to become aware of these emotional patterns and realize that there are other ways to respond to life that are healthier and more natural. However, as with any addiction, giving up drama and suffering can be tricky – if all our relationships

have been filled with drama in the past, it is hard to believe that relationships without drama can be real. The good news is that as you integrate your wounded aspects, you will naturally find yourself slipping away from drama. Once you've had an experience of no-drama in your life, you'll never miss the old days (well, you might miss them a little bit – but instead of inviting chaos into your life, you realize that watching drama on a stage or on a screen is a much more graceful way to enjoy it. Also, you realize that you can have *adventure* and feelings without having drama).

2.   **Relationships**: Aah, human relationships. Everything in life revolves around relationships – they determine whether you are having a good day, they help or hinder your survival, and they can turn life into heaven or hell. Of course, it's possible to have relationships without the drama factor, and in that case, they can be integrated into the experience of embodied enlightenment. The fact is, however, that most of us choosing enlightenment in this lifetime come to face a very difficult choice at least once on this path: Whether to hold onto an old, dear relationship despite knowing that it will pull us back from our own sovereignty, or whether to move into our freedom with the knowingness that we must release that old relationship. It is not uncommon to put off enlightenment for lifetimes, just because the heart is not yet ready to let go. What I am noticing, though, is that the more I am in integrity with myself, the more I attract people into my life that support my sovereignty rather than limit it.

3.   **Ancestors**: Perhaps you're not aware of how much your ancestors affect your everyday-reality. But they do. First of all, your entire biology is geared towards securing two goals:

1) To survive as long as possible, and 2) to procreate and thus continue the ancestral lineage. Note that our bodies are not conditioned for living creative, fulfilled, peaceful lives. The fact that we are intelligent, thinking humans, doesn't exempt us from this inherited biological programming. In addition to inheriting our DNA and the obsessive strive to survive from our ancestors, we also inherit a wide range of psychological conditions and belief systems: This includes highly subconscious beliefs, attitudes and perceptions as well as patterns of behaviour.

Thus it is fair to say that our bond to our ancestral lineage holds us back from stepping into sovereignty – unless we make a very clear and conscious choice to release this bond. It is important to note that releasing your ancestral lineage can be done in full honour and gratitude for what they have provided. Understand that this choice will feel very strange to yourself and your family and might be encountered with resistance. This is an energetic choice, not something that you need to be verbal about – ultimately, it's just about you choosing your freedom on every level, including the biological stratum.

4.   **The Mind**: How easy awakening would be if it wasn't for the mind! The fear of going crazy and losing mental control is a very common obstacle at the threshold of enlightenment. Of course, it doesn't help that we live in a society that values the intellect more than anything and is built around the assumption that we need to control our lives, our surroundings and ourselves. The mind loves patterns, control and predictability, so it will rebel against things like freedom, magic, trust, etc. Chances are, though, that it is your mind that will drive you crazy – not the act of going beyond the mind. And yet you

can't allow enlightenment without also allowing yourself to go beyond the obsessions of the mind. When you find yourself in that tight, tense, stressful place where your thoughts are spinning like mad, my advice is to relax. If you think that's too easy, believe me, in that moment it will not feel easy. However, if you can just allow yourself to relax physically, emotionally and mentally (in other words, let go of control altogether for a few minutes) then your mind can "breathe", and that's when your consciousness flows through your mind to rebalance it. If you don't know how to relax, play a recording of a guided breathing or relaxation audio – but make sure to choose one that you really do find relaxing[12].

5.   **Addiction to Self-Improvement**: The question is, do you really want enlightenment, or do you want to continue being the spiritual seeker? Becoming conscious of our flaws and shortcomings is the first step into awakening, but often this quest for self-improvement turns into an obsessive compulsion along the way, because the search for perfection is addictive. But have you considered that every time you try to improve yourself, you are basically affirming that there's something wrong with you? The ascended masters tell us that enlightenment is total self-acceptance; sooner or later, we must give up self-improvement to make space for self-acceptance.

6.   **Not Feeling Safe**: Integration – which basically is enlightenment in action – can only happen to the extent that we feel safe within ourselves. There is a difference between feeling safe and not feeling fear: You can feel fear and still be

---

12   You might want to try Norma Delaney's guided breathing: www. compassionatebreath.net/.

in your safe space by observing the fear and realizing that the fear is only a small part of your experience. Creating the safe space means being connected to your soul. This metaphysical act of choosing the safe space will affect your physical reality, and obviously taking care of your physical reality will make it easier for you to access your "spiritual" safe space. If you are struggling with feelings of fear and anxiety, start connecting to the sensuality of yourself and to the sensuality of being alive. The reason for this is that true sensuality (which requires an openness and intimacy with self) has a very similar energetic frequency to unconditional love and to the feeling of safety. The safer we feel physically, emotionally and psychically, the easier it will be to allow enlightenment.

7.   **Lack of Abundance**: If you are experiencing lack of abundance, it's easy to see this as an obstacle to enlightenment, because we associate money with freedom (and of course, on this physical plane, money is necessary if we want to engage in society). But the truth is, if there is lack, it's there for a reason. If you are experiencing lack, you can always use this opportunity to integrate any fears you have around financial lack and to breathe with any resistance you feel towards your current situation. In other words, you can acknowledge that *everything* in your life, even the content (or lack of content) of your bank account serves your enlightenment.

8.   **Health Issues**: A big part of awakening is releasing old patterns – including physical and physiological patterns. Naturally these deep changes will affect your health. Although eventually your health will be much more balanced, the short-term reality might appear very different. There's quite a fine line between allowing your light-body to integrate with the

physical body, and exploding the circuits, so to speak. These changes that happen electro-magnetically and later on a cellular level can be very intense: Skin rashes, allergies, asthma, nausea, vertigo, chronic fatigue, violent coughs and headaches are some of the symptoms that I've experienced due to this process (but these can vary from person to person). Although some level of physical discomfort is inevitable as you release heaps of stuck energies, getting a terminal disease is not necessary. What you can do to support your physical balance is to get enough rest, drink lots of water, do conscious breathing on a daily basis and some light physical exercise such as walking, dancing, swimming or yoga.

9.   **Spiritual Teachings**: All the New Age methods, techniques, therapies and theories help you very little when you come face to face with your own shadows. Most of the teachings available are just another attempt to control the mind, to escape the feelings, to get more energy or to fill the hungry void within us. Just because someone calls himself a spiritual teacher does not mean that you should trust him more than you trust yourself (and especially your soul). Being sovereign doesn't mean that you can't accept help from the outside – on the contrary, a sovereign master allows herself/himself to receive abundant support. But when you do come across a spiritual teaching, take it with a grain of salt, or rather, with a grain of intuition, and check with your inner guidance: Does this teaching support me or not? Is this relevant for me right now? Your soul has a remarkably accurate radar for detecting distraction, but you must take that quiet moment to hear the soul-voice beneath all the distracting mind-chatter.

10. **Shame and Guilt**: Last, but not least, there is the issue of shame and guilt. The weight of these shadow aspects can be very heavy, and ultimately you will have to let go of them and *radically forgive yourself everything* if you choose to walk on to enlightenment.

I call these obstacles 'distractions', because although some of them might seem insurmountable, they will only hold onto you as long as you hold onto them. Until one day, you are ready to simply take the next step and walk on without looking back.

The Last Veil

~ Limitations are an illusion, and illusion itself is the greatest of limitations. ~

On the way to enlightenment, you will sooner or later come face to face with the question of power, the last veil of illusion. Power is the deepest belief that separates you from your divinity, and all other veils of illusion, *maya*[13], depend on this one. The belief in power, in duality, in good and evil, are all different versions of the same veil. 'Evil' is nothing but a veil of separation; nothing more than a belief that you are separate from the divine.

Power only exists in the realm of the mind. As long as you believe that evil exists, a part of you is stuck in the perspective of duality; if you play the game of duality, you also play the

---

13   Maya is an Eastern term meaning the "world's illusion". Those who seek true liberation from suffering, caused by the veils of illusion, must learn to see with their inner vision.

game of power. When you play the game of power, you get stuck in roles such as victim or villain. In other words, you are only free once you have walked beyond the power dynamic altogether: Only someone who is still playing the power-game has a need and desire for power. You cannot control power by becoming more powerful; you cannot play with power without being played by power.

Another way to say it is that you are never truly a victim of another person, but you may be a victim of power acting through you and through other people. Power is based on the belief that you are limited instead of a sovereign creator; once you truly step out of that core belief, you will never feel the need or desire to use power anymore.

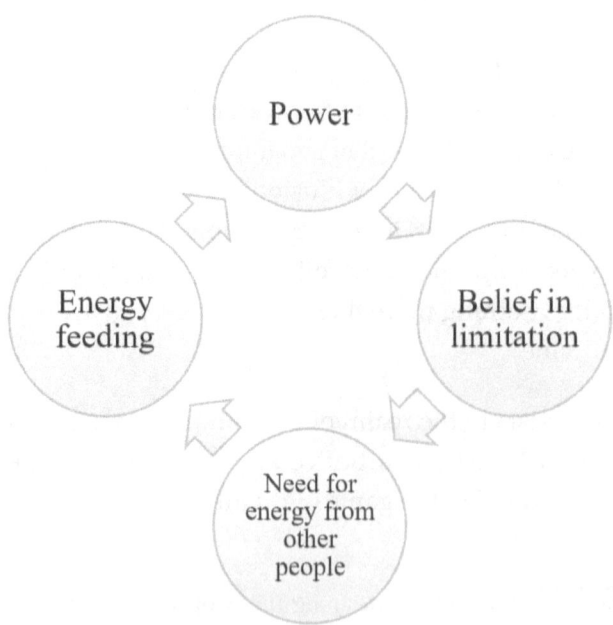

To step outside of the power-matrix, you have to let go of the belief in any evil, and to let go of the belief that power affects you. Power is never an absolute, but always temporary, that is to say, in a Buddhist sense, it is an illusion – a powerful illusion, but only if you believe in it and fear it. You will never find lasting satisfaction through power, because power is inherently always in a state of battle. The illusion of power has no power over you once you realize that it is an illusion. To walk beyond power means releasing your victim-identity, and letting go of your martyr, saint, and abuser-identities as well. It means allowing yourself to release any beliefs about you having ever done anything wrong or bad. This includes forgiving yourself for your humanity with all its imperfections, and forgiving yourself for all the suffering that you have experienced as a result of being human. It is realizing that all of us have aspects coloured in all the shades of grey and that's okay. And finally, it is realizing that there is nothing to forgive, because you never sinned. You always have been and always are pure, worthy, and clear. This is freedom at its purest.

Very often the words 'freedom' and 'power' are confused with each other or even used synonymously. Those who seek power do so because they believe power is their ticket to freedom, which means safety. The ultimate need of the power-hungry, and we've all been hungry for power at some point, is to control the external world in an attempt to feel safe. The more addicted one is to power, the less safe he or she feels. Once she has achieved a momentary state of power, she feels safe – but only for an instant, because soon her power will the threatened by others who seek power.

Freedom, however, is the antithesis of power: Only someone who is free doesn't need power, and only someone who has let go of power, is free. In fact, power is a twisted, synthetic substitute for freedom. Power is sold and marketed as freedom, yet they are as different as oil and water. Power is fuelled by illusion and is acquired through control, whereas freedom is inherent (meaning that ultimately it cannot be lost or gained) and only becomes apparent through the absence of control. Freedom is the state of ultimate, eternal safety. A state of such deep self-trust that no matter what happens on the external level, we know that we exist eternally. It is a constant underlying current that we cannot see, feel, or acknowledge as long as we are attached to power. The person who seeks power, believes that freedom is found in the external world. By controlling the external, she will have more freedom – or so she believes.

The person who is free understands that freedom can only be permanent once it is found within. Not by controlling the inner feelings and thoughts (that would be applying power to our internal self), but simply by acknowledging the space between the emotions and the thoughts, by sensing the stillness, the expansiveness within, around and beyond the noise. In this expansive stillness, or emptiness as the Buddhists call it, we realize that we don't need to free ourselves – we are already free, have always been and will always be free. That is our true nature. But this realization is nothing but an intellectual concept, until we have the courage to go beyond power by accepting others and ourselves as we are.

True freedom doesn't mean being free of external limitations; chances are you will not be able to walk through walls but still need to open doors as a free human, and you probably will also need to eat something to feel nourished and vitalised. Freedom then refers to the ability to perceive the free dimension of yourself beneath the dimension of physical reality, and even beneath the reality of thoughts and emotions. The physical dimension and also the dimension of thoughts and emotions are filled with limits and limitations – we are not trying to change that. In freedom, we are simply expanding our awareness to include a perspective beyond the limitations.

Freedom can't be reached from a place of fear, because it's the opposite vibration of fear. So what to do when you feel fear? You accept it as it is: Yes, there is a feeling of fear that limits your experience AND, at the same time, you assume and eventually know that there is a limitless dimension within yourself that doesn't fear. Even if you can't feel that invisible, free dimension, you can still open up to it. You can say, I believe in this possibility of freedom and I'm curious enough to open myself to explore this more.

~ When you relax, you let go of control. And letting go of control is the last step before enlightenment. ~

Walking beyond power means walking beyond the need to push, force, or control anything or anyone. It can feel strange at first, but when you allow yourself to see yourself through soul's eyes, to remember your true essence and radiance, you realize that power is just a game. It is a chess game that you have played with such conviction that it has become real, but it doesn't need to be your reality. One of the best-kept secrets of this world is that reality is flexible – it is what you allow it to be. Walking beyond power means letting go of the fight within you and with other people, but especially against yourself.

What is at the core of all power struggles, whether or not we are aware of that, is the battle between the inner masculine and the inner feminine parts of us. When there is control and fear and lack of trust between the masculine and the feminine within, then this conflict will be reflected back to us through external power struggles. It doesn't matter what our gender or sexual orientation is, we each have the inner masculine and feminine within us. It is not about strengthening one in relation to the other, but strengthening and healing each in relation to itself. Only unconditional love can restore this inner balance. Through unconditional self-love, the masculine learns to accept himself as he is, and the feminine learns to accept herself as she is. In this way the relation between these two aspects within us naturally comes into harmony. If we have not allowed this full acceptance of both aspects of self, then we will relate to other people's wounded aspects through the filters of our wounded aspects; as opposed to relating to the conscious being standing in front of us through our own conscious beingness.

Once you end the battles within, you no longer attract people into your life that play with power. And even if they do walk through your life, their power doesn't touch you – it's as if you become invisible to power. What makes it safe to let go of power, to let go of control? Self-love. This brings us to the last frontier of the awakening human: Allowing the love for self unconditionally, irrevocably, and completely.

The Freedom of Self-Love

~ All spiritual paths eventually lead to self-love. ~

Perhaps the most difficult thing a human will ever do is to love oneself, a wise friend and teacher once said. Loving yourself is almost synonymous with enlightenment, and the reason why so few humans have ascended. It's hard, because in order to fully love yourself, you first have to heal the wounds of past love relationships, and to clear any questions regarding love on behalf of your soul. Until you integrate your love-aspects, there will always be a hesitation, resistance, fear or manipulation in your love, both in relationship to yourself and to others. In addition, your aspects are trained to either serve others or to serve your ego, but very rarely to truly serve yourself. Self-love is also hard because it requires forgiving ourselves for our mistakes and accepting all our imperfections. Because we have lived with ourselves our whole lives, we are intimately aware of our shortcomings. On top of this, we have very few role models of self-love, which is why the concept might feel very strange. Lastly, there is also societal conditioning of "loving thy neighbour first", meaning that we idolize martyrdom and expect a "good person", especially in the case of a woman, to put everyone else's needs in front of her own.

In her book, *The Voice of the Silence*, H.P. Blavatsky refers to two distinct paths to liberation: The Doctrine of the Eye, and the Doctrine of the Heart. The former one, which is practiced by the followers of Theravada Buddhism for example, claims that one can only save oneself, no others. In contrast, the followers of Mahayana Buddhism, amongst others, choose to remain in the world to help others find liberation from suffering as well. This Doctrine of the Heart, also called the Bodhisattva Path, is the one suggested by Madame Blavatsky herself. And yet I question, why not integrate the Doctrine of the Eye and the Heart? Is there really a separation between liberating oneself of suffering and helping others to do the same? Will the mere act of choosing our own liberation, and staying here on Earth embodying our free state of being not convince others that liberation from suffering is in fact possible? There are many paths to freedom, and I can only choose my own path. My experience is that we cannot save each other, but we can definitely support each other on this path. In addition, I believe this support is only as genuine and helpful as the depth of our inner freedom. Until we at least glimpse our inner vision (as the Doctrine of the Eye teaches), how can we know that our actions from the heart (the Doctrine of the Heart) are unconditional, rather than merely satisfying our human need to be recognized as a "good person". My intention here is to point out that there are more than just two paths to liberation, and every one of those paths can potentially lead us into more illusions or into illumination, depending on our clarity and our intentions.

For me, the issue to focus on is not whether self-love or universal love is the key. The key is in neither of these concepts, but in the unconditional nature with which we practice either one, or both. One cannot truly be without the other; if we practice loving the world and every person we encounter unconditionally, we will arrive at self-love. One the other hand, loving oneself unconditionally will naturally expand our love for others. When I started this path of awakening, I directed my love outside of me. This eventually brought me to a place, where I literally had to start loving myself if I wanted to survive. That is the reason why I tend to emphasise love for self, first, but please remember that you are free to choose your path. Each of us will encounter the experiences that we need in order to realize what we have come here to realize.

What does it take to love oneself? Before you can receive love from yourself, you have to clear your concept of 'love' from the tainted meanings it has been draped with throughout your many experiences. To so many of us, love has come to mean rules, possession, pain, drama and sacrifice. We have forgotten its true nature, which is free, innocent, and allowing. When you love someone completely (and you can only love someone completely when you have released your fears about love) then you allow that person anything – not out of fearful compromise, but you will allow her anything because that comes easily and naturally to you. When you really see the God within another being, why wouldn't you allow him anything he desired? It doesn't mean that you have to be together with this person if it doesn't feel good for you or that you should continue spending time with people who abuse you or drain your energies, it simply means that you honour his or her every choice from the bottom of your heart (just as you also honour your own truth).

Of course, this is not what we have been taught; on the contrary, we have learned that love supposedly means owning, limiting and expecting things from the other person. We have learned that suffering and judging ourselves are virtues. None of that, however, is love; it might be a drop of pure love mixed with a lot of confusion and lack of awareness. Perhaps a part of you loves another person unconditionally, but if there are other aspects within you that are ruled by fear, that love is not clear; it's conditional, meaning that it is diluted with power. Please don't judge yourself if your love is infused with fear, as it nearly always is in human relationships. It simply means that you are carrying some old fears that can be integrated and released. It takes a huge amount of courage to let go of those old fears, but on the other hand, keeping those fears will eventually exhaust you to death if you're not ready to let go of them voluntarily. Why not become aware of your beliefs and feelings about love, and then you can release any fears attached to love, *gently and persistently*.

Sometimes when we fall in love with someone, we are really falling in love with a lost part of ourselves that becomes visible to us through another person or through our connection with that person. This is especially the case with relationships that are very karmic, intense and challenging. One of the reasons why break-ups are so painful is that we feel as if we have lost a part of ourselves. Yet from the wider perspective, you can never lose something that is truly yours. You can only lose sight of it. So if you feel that deep longing for a soulmate, consider if this is perhaps in fact an intense longing to be present with your authentic Self.

In contemporary spiritual literature, there is much controversy about the topic of self-love. As I see it, it's not a choice between loving yourself versus loving other people and being loved by others. It's a choice between exploring self-love versus not exploring it on a conscious level. Your self-love is never, ever away from the love that you can give to or receive from others – if it is, we are not talking about love. If you don't know where to start regarding self-love, know that your soul is the manifestation of pure self-love. Your soul loves you without any limitations, so if you feel clueless in this area, ask soul directly to show you what self-love feels like. Here are some other suggestions to help you explore self-love in practice:

• *Allow yourself to enjoy life*. Stop trying to be so goddamn perfect and have some fun! You know, *sex, magic & rock'n'roll*. Or whatever fun means for you. We have to get over this idea that suffering is noble. If you've forgotten what the word 'fun' stands for (it sometimes happens on this path), it's about joy, playfulness, entertainment, amusement, pleasure and delight. Do something ridiculous, or even outrageous. Do something that makes you laugh. Smile at yourself in the mirror. Pamper yourself. Surprise yourself. Be spontaneous. Do something completely unnecessary for the sheer pleasure of it. Find out, what makes your heart sing? What makes you dance with excitement? What inspires you? What made you smile today? What makes you fall in love with life? The spiritual path is a deep endeavour, but there are times when the most spiritual thing you can do for yourself is just to have a good laugh. When you love life, loving yourself will follow naturally.

- *Be real with yourself.* In the end, other people don't care very much about how you appear to the world. Being authentic and honest in your relationships will save you so much trouble, but the one thing that really matters is how authentic you are with yourself. Authenticity requires courage, especially emotional courage, but once you allow yourself to see, feel and be aware of what's going on within you, what your needs and desires are right now, you are in a position where you can start to have compassion for yourself as you are in this moment. Journaling is a great tool to discover your authentic self.

- *Be present with yourself.* Perhaps one of the simplest, yet most transformative spiritual practices is to just take a moment each day to *be* present with yourself: To do this, choose a place and time disconnected from/undisturbed by other people, and feel your own presence like you would feel the presence of a dear friend. Observe any thoughts or emotions, without trying to change them, and relax into your own company. You can do this practice with closed eyes or open eyes. You can do this at home, or while walking in nature. If you get distracted, gently pull your attention back to yourself. Whether you call this meditation, allowing, conscious breathing or something else, it's simply about being attentive to yourself. The purpose of this experience is to help you become aware of your ever-present soul connection, which is the actual source of self-love (and love for others).

It's also about *beingness*: Experiencing, sensing and feeling yourself without having to do any activity. After a while, you'll be able to be present with yourself even in the company of other people. You can also consciously practice feeling your own presence when you interact with others. For example, if you have a lover, you can remember to feel your own presence while sharing an intimate moment with your partner. The more present you are with yourself, the more present you can be with other people as well. For women it is especially helpful to be present in their physical bodies, whereas for men, it's to be present in their heart area and with their feelings. Your presence is one of the most valuable and beautiful gifts that you can give to yourself and to others.

• *Open up to yourself, to life and to sensuality.* When we fall in love, our hearts are wide open. It's a very receptive, raw, expansive, and sensual state. We want to get close and intimate with the other person; we almost want to lose ourselves in that intense connection. It really is possible to experience that kind of intimate connection with yourself. When you allow yourself to feel and get close to all parts of yourself, to fully open up to your natural, free, unrestricted self, the love will start flowing in. When you choose enlightenment, you don't integrate just the dark aspects; you also integrate aspects that were previously hidden because they were so sensual that it wasn't safe for them to be expressed. However, once you start to feel safe with yourself, you are ready to open up to your sensual nature again.

• *Be your own best friend and lover.* How do you treat someone that you deeply and unconditionally love? That can give you some ideas how to start loving yourself. For example, take a mirror and look yourself deeply into the eyes, with complete acceptance and compassion. Caress your face and touch yourself like you would touch a lover. Ask yourself every day how you feel, what you need and what you desire. Say beautiful things to yourself and about yourself. Wear clothes that make you feel really good… Self-love isn't complicated; it just feels strange at first because humans have lost touch with themselves.

"Loving yourself truly requires no effort whatsoever, just allowing."
Adamus Saint-Germain

If you are here for enlightenment, you could forget about all the other teachings and only focus on self-love: It is through self-love that your fragmented aspects are integrated, it is through self-love that you learn to listen to your intuition, it is through self-love that you let go of power. Similarly, it can be said that all the other tips and techniques presented in this book will bring you closer to self-love. In the end, you cannot escape self-love – it will wait for you at the end of any and every spiritual path, even the Bodhisattva Path. And when you find it, you will realize that *self-love is freedom at the deepest level.*

What Is Enlightenment Anyway?

The joke is that *enlightenment is, anyway.* You are already enlightened, and now you are simply witnessing the unfolding of how the human self allows this free perspective of you, the soul, to be fully realized and embodied here on Earth. Enlightenment is the realization of the timeless principle: "As above, so below". What does it take to accept heaven to integrate with the earthly self? That is the natural unfolding that you are witnessing and experiencing.

Realization is timeless, but the human within us generally requires time before it is ready to accept its true timeless nature. Your essence was never wounded, but your human aspect may need some healing before it is ready to accept its wholeness. Your soul is already wise, but you, the human, might need years of study before you recognize the insignificance of studying. The funny thing is, we don't need to learn or grow our way into enlightenment, yet it usually is through learning that we reach the readiness to give up the game of learning, healing and maturing. The paradox of being a divine human is that we walk the path in order to see its illusion: from a "higher" perspective, there is no start or end to this journey. There is no necessary minimum amount of time that needs to pass before one can allow enlightenment. There's nowhere to go either, because all the action is happening right here, right now. In other words, realization will come to you; you cannot go to it.

Most of us who are awakening have spent many lifetimes here on Earth. The lifetime of your ascension is different from any other lifetime you've lived, because the focus is not on gaining more wisdom and more perspective but rather on bringing all your past experiences together into one distilled circle of completion. Each of your "past" lives is like a story that is complete save for the last chapter – and your self-designated mission for this lifetime is to finish every one of those stories. The last chapter of each story holds great significance, because it is the chapter that gives resolution to the entire storyline; it's the chapter that gives meaning to a perhaps messy and incomprehensible plot. Although this significant task might feel like a burden of responsibility at times, it is a natural process led by your soul.

There are many things one could say about enlightenment, ascension or self-realization: It's a completion but not an end.

It's freedom from illusion. It's not a problem-free zone, but it's a judgement-free, power-free, graceful and energy-rich zone. It's the traveller finding home within himself. It's God remembering his/her own divinity. It's consciousness becoming aware of itself. It's knowingness recognizing its own wisdom. It's when the sovereign being realizes its inherent freedom.

~ Enlightenment is the ultimate destiny and destination of every Souled being. It's the original dream. And what's more: it is real and very possible. ~

Of course, realization is way beyond words and mental concepts. However, the human aspect within us likes to hear something concrete, even if it's just a shadow of the real experience. That's why I asked my future fully realized Self to write me a letter about it:

Dear younger Self,

You ask yourself what enlightenment is, and how long it will take for you to get there... You will neither become less human, nor a more perfect human. You will become more open as a human, while becoming more aware of the other dimensions of yourself. You will start to express more of your free Self. You will lead a life on many levels at the same time. You will be more present in your life than ever before, more sensually open to the experience of life. At the same time, you will be more distant from it than before, because now you are aware of a more expanded perspective, one in which human life is merely one layer of your experience of reality, almost a distraction, a show, a story to spice up your true essence, which is consciousness. You will live half a dimension away, or in other words, in many dimensions simultaneously. You will be less attached to human things, like emotions and relationships, yet more acutely aware of the beauty and sacredness of every little detail of human life. You will be an observer of your human self, while diving deeply into the human experiences. You will start enjoying the synchronicities of life, which have always been there, but now you are in tune with them rather than in resistance to them.

You will find magic in silence, in simplicity and in nothingness. That is how you balance yourself. You will always return to this core, this core that is so expanded, you can hardly call it just a core. It is a space where no limitations, no attachments and no relations define you. Where you are free. You will bring this freedom into your human life as well, as you let go of fear. You are already tapping into this, into the act of allowing. It is saying Yes to life. Not to avoid death, not to be more successful than someone else, not because someone expects this from you, but simply saying Yes for the passion of being, feeling and expressing! Not holding back anymore, finally released from the past. And then the energies will flow. First you will have a tendency to limit the flow, out of habit. But soon you will start to remember that there is nothing to hold onto, because there is nothing that you can actually lose.

Everything you need already exists and comes to you as appropriate, without a shimmer of effort. Once you allow yourself to connect with your multidimensional Self, to All of you, once you discover your sovereign domain, your inner kingdom, then the rest will follow. Start with trust: total, undeniable trust in your own clarity, freedom, and existence. For now, just relax, release whatever is not yours and receive the gifts that soul has to offer you. And dear human, allow yourself to laugh often and outrageously. The secret is that anything, including enlightenment, is just a breath away. Until you choose to realize it in the now moment…

With love, your "future" Self.

Part 3

Life After Awakening

Living in Mastery

What is spiritual mastery? What is your definition of mastery? Take a moment to feel into it. Traditionally, a master is seen as one who has survived the death of her ego. However, this classical definition can be misleading, as it implies a battle that is fought against the ego. Often a master is depicted as an avatar who masters his thoughts, emotions and his physical body. Again, this definition implies control, force and judgment. I've personally never met a master who applies control on his or her thoughts and emotions. The idea that mastery is battle that you win against your ego is in itself very dualistic and limited. In addition, I feel it is time to realize that mastery doesn't mean conquering the weak human aspects within ourselves. Perhaps the ego never dies as long as we are human, but it softly integrates into the expanded space of the self-loving being that we are becoming. What is dying in self-realization is an old perception of ourselves as the ego.

When I talk about masters, I am referring to embodied or ascended beings who have recognized the master within and who speak with the voice of their inner master. A master isn't necessarily a spiritual teacher; he or she might have students, but that isn't the defining factor. Furthermore, I don't see masters as spiritual supermen and wonder women, or as embodiments of perfection. What makes someone a master, as I define it, is recognizing and accepting the master within. A master could be a young woman who is a waitress at a coffee shop, but if she has walked down the path of self-discovery, and walked far enough to face her shadows and walked even beyond that to face her inner master, and has dared to invite this inner master to participate in her life despite her human imperfections – that is a master to me. Not a title bestowed by others, but a realization that emerges through the encounter with the free self.

Mastery is the result of integrating the insights of awakening and applying them in everyday life. After awakening, you'll continue to expand and experience and express yourself. You will continue to find out more about who you are, and you will continue to fall deeper in love with yourself, and with others and with life. The difference is, that you will live from the perspective of your sovereign self; you will live *because you can*, rather than live because you must survive. Mastery is closely linked to your enlightenment, but you certainly don't have to wait for enlightenment to practice mastery!

Why Creating Your Reality is a Reality

As a master, you perceive yourself as a creator. You also perceive everyone else as creators, whether they themselves are conscious of being creators or not. On this spiritual path, many of us come across the concept of manifestation and the law of attraction: The idea, that as conscious creators of our reality, we should be able to manifest the life we want. Manifestation is a part of mastery, but it isn't the point of mastery or the most significant aspect of it. However, I will address it here, because I remember having many questions related to this, and even being distracted by these concepts. Magical phenomena and miraculous manifestations are real and possible, however, if that is the main motivation for you to explore this path, you are walking a path of power rather than freedom, and that is your choice to make.[14]

The number of spiritual teachers and self-help authors who have attempted to teach the concept of conscious manifestation is so high that now there is a vast amount of highly contradictory, perplexing and misleading information available at just a few clicks of the keyboard. As always, when reading this text and other authors, please remember *discernment* – that inner voice of clarity, intuition and just plain common sense. Let's take a look at the dynamics of creation and manifestation, which are often misunderstood.

As you know, life doesn't just ambiguously "happen" – it's created. Your reality is a co-creation between your human personality and the free soul-self, who has gathered wisdom from all your lifetimes, interacting with the rest of the world. What makes this whole endeavour complex is that your human personality isn't just one aspect, but consists of innumerable aspects that are mostly subconscious and highly conditioned to act in societally accepted patterns. So now imagine this compilation of subconscious aspects (each with their own agenda), your partly conscious human identity plus your divine self joining forces to interact with a bunch of other souled beings in a dense and limited planet that operates on the law of attraction. Is it a wonder that we have a lot of chaos around us? Especially when the vast majority of humanity has no idea how creation works? Now we can understand why it feels like a lot of different, seemingly random factors contribute to the creation of external reality.

---

14   In the Mahatma Letters, master Koot Hoomi lal Singh expands on this subject to the theosophist A. P. Sinnett.

Starting from which family and which set of genes we are born into, the basics of our life are designed long before we enter the body of the infant who is to become our human identity. The more conscious we are about the dynamics of creation, the more freedom we have for choosing the direction our life takes. We could go into all the energy physics of how the law of attraction works, but it's not necessary – we don't need to understand quantum physics or the metaphysical laws of energy to create consciously.

Let's distil these concepts into what really matters: You are a sovereign creator, and it is your choice whether to react to life and see it as something done to you, or to acknowledge your inherent creatorship and see yourself as a creative channel for life. It is the *perception of yourself* as a creator that will create real change and shift your experience from being a prisoner of life to being an artist and designer of life. In many ways, sovereignty is what some people call 'empowerment', with the difference that sovereignty in this sense includes the spiritual dimension: We can own our freedom, in all dimensions of our existence. This might feel very uncomfortable at first, because it means shifting the role of creatorship from an external, omnipotent God onto yourself. In other words, taking full responsibility of your destiny means acknowledging your divinity – and if you come from a religious background, hardly anything could feel more blasphemous. Religion, ironically, can really hold you back in your awakening. There's no way getting around it: Stepping into your mastery, and believing that you're a sinful human who is dependent on some authoritative, elusive God, are mutually exclusive perspectives. Sovereignty is seeing the God within you, and the God within everyone else, and that's only possible when we give up the belief in God as something that exists outside of us.

Sovereignty, which is synonymous with mastery, is the basis of conscious creation and manifestation. The critical thing to understand about sovereignty is that it's not realized in relation to other humans. This seems strange to us as a social species, but it's one of the rare things that we can only experience and realize in relation to ourselves. In other words, you don't learn about your sovereignty by comparing yourself to other humans who may be more or less sovereign than you. You can only learn about true sovereignty in relation to yourself, and through the relationship that you have with yourself, and through your inner experiences. In sovereignty, there is no perception of superiority or inferiority; there is merely awareness and lack of awareness. It's important to understand that sovereignty is not another advancement on the ladder of spiritual superiority; in fact, the essence of sovereignty is the stepping outside of all hierarchical or dualistic perceptions.

Of course, you don't shift into the perspective of being a creator overnight even if you're fully committed to sovereignty, but there are certain things you can immediately practice and apply in your current life, if you choose. Whilst acknowledging your inherent creatorship is very liberating, I would caution against doing it for the purpose of becoming a master-manifestor; self-realization isn't about alchemizing metal into gold. Whenever I feel a strong desire to change something in my life, I first ask myself *why* do I want to create that, and which part within me has this desire. For example, if I want to manifest a partner into my life because I feel incomplete without one, perhaps the important thing is for me to consciously love myself and to address those feelings of incompleteness and lack of self-worth. The point is, you can use the perspective of creatorship to support your mastery, or you can use it as a spiritual bypass tool. Whatever your choice is, be aware of it.

How to Shift Into the Perspective of Creatorship

We don't need to learn how to do conscious creating; we only need to learn how to step out of the way of our natural creative essence. Sometimes our creations turn out very different from what we would like them to be, despite us owning the fact that we are conscious creators. There are several reasons why this is the case, as discussed below.

a)   We are sovereign, free beings – and so is everyone else. The first step into conscious creatorship is to accept that we can't expect other people or life to be the way we would like them to be. We are only ever free to change ourselves. When we create consciously, it's very important to create for ourselves. Whenever we try to create something for another person, we are in fact dismissing their sovereignty, instead of acknowledging them as equally free and sovereign beings. It is one thing to send unconditional love to someone, and quite another thing to try to manifest a relationship with a specific person without asking this person whether he or she actually wants to be involved. Thus it can be said that conscious creatorship starts with accepting what is – within us and around us.

b)   Sometimes there is a part of you that holds you back because it doesn't want things to go the way you consciously think you want them to go. When you find yourself stuck in old patterns, the chances are that a wounded aspect within you is calling for your attention and wants to be healed. In an attempt to heal itself, it creates a repetition of the circumstances that caused the wound, hoping that this time you would resolve the situation in a new way and find *resolution*. For example, if you felt like an outsider as a small child but were not able to process that emotion at the time, your inner child is now staging a re-enactment of the trauma by creating an experience of isolation, so that you, the adult, can rewrite a healing ending to the story. Then your inner child will feel liberated and can finally grow up to join you in your mature state. Whenever there is a persistent pattern in your life, it's because the pattern wants to find completion, but needs your conscious attention to do that. Conscious creation only works when we create from our whole self. One ignored aspect can be enough to distort a harmonious outcome. We can compare conscious creation to an orchestra: Our conscious self, the conductor, needs to make sure that all the aspects, like the individual musicians, are aligned and playing to the same rhythm. If one musician is out of tune, we need to take a break and address this aspect.

c)   Another reason why *seemingly* stupid things happen to us despite all our human efforts is that our soul-desires impact our lives, but they often are disconnected from our human identity. They might be out of alignment because your soul-desires are your deepest, truest desires and what I call 'human desires' are what the ego thinks are your desires, but really are just attempts to avoid discomfort. Soul-desires are usually about experiencing the depth, sensuality, beauty and colour of life, and also about creativity and self-expression. In contrast, human desires are usually about achieving goals, being successful, being liked by others and feeling secure emotionally, mentally, physically, socially and financially. Do you dare to choose the path less travelled?

Your soul, and remember that *you are your soul*, has a wider perspective than your human mind, and it doesn't distinguish between good and bad experiences. It just wants to experience, expand and express through you, the conscious human. You see, whenever you experience, your consciousness expands, and this is the passion of the soul – regardless of what the experience was. Think about it: whenever you have a challenging experience, you find out more about who you are, and what you are not. You find out more about what you like, and don't like. From a soul-perspective, some of the darkest experiences of the human are the most sacred, because they have brought so much wisdom, depth and compassion to you – only someone who has experienced pain understands love; only someone who has been powerless understands the value of freedom! Consider perceiving the situation through the eyes of your soul-self.

Sometimes trauma is also a way for soul to reconnect with the human in a more embodied way. This is because trauma tends to momentarily tear down all the walls of defence mechanisms, so that the soul can get through to the human. As Eckhart Tolle has said, the bad things in life are the best things for your spirituality. I don't believe this to be the case always, but sometimes it is. This is why your human self might like nothing more than comfort, success and a cool identity, whereas the master within you has grander desires. That being said, your soul always has your best interest at heart, because essentially it is you. Your human personality is free to suppress and ignore the soul-desires, but usually the consequences are grim because your soul actually does know what's best for you. You can get in touch with your soul-desires by 1) being very authentic with yourself, 2) listening to you heart, 3) following your joy, 4) loving yourself, 5) noticing what works well for you, 6) noticing what fills you with energy, inspiration or peace of mind, and 7) by releasing that which drains your energy and joy.

The one thing that is always left for you to try, even if nothing else has worked, is trusting your soul: Trust, that even when you can't possibly see how this situation is serving you, somehow it is exactly what you need right now. Something that may seem like an obstacle or inconvenience to you, could in fact be your soul leading you along a secret short-cut to your authentic wellbeing and bliss. Trusting your soul means letting your inner wisdom conduct your life, rather than the desires of your ego. When you trust that all is well, all really becomes well in your personal life (not perfect, but well), no matter what is happening in the world at large.

d)   We must also understand that the path of awakening is a path of freedom. Not conditional freedom, or external freedom, but total freedom regardless of the external circumstances. As long as we expect an external condition, such as the right partner or the right job, to fulfil us, we are not free. As long as we set conditions on our own freedom, we will never know true freedom. This is not to suggest that you ought to give up your dreams and desires, but rather to confirm that if you find yourself losing everything you were attached to, there is a reason for it – consider that perhaps your soul is guiding you towards real freedom.

e)   The final reason why sometimes things don't happen

gracefully, despite us practicing conscious creatorship, is that we are in a process of transformation. After perceiving ourselves as victims of our circumstances for most of our lifetime(s), it takes some serious practice to see ourselves as creators. Don't give up and don't give in to frustration. Be patient with yourself, be patient with the process, and ask for help when you need it. Involve your friends and family in your transition by asking them to encourage you to take responsibility, and surround yourself with people, nature, books, and other materials that inspire and support you. Keep away from people who discourage you, at least until you feel more stable on your feet as you practice masterful energy management[15] and conscious creation.

Now we can explore some practical steps that you can take to remember your natural creator abilities:

1.   The first thing is to let go of blame. Truly, *do not blame anyone, including yourself, for anything*. This has to do with stepping into our sovereignty and taking responsibility for our creations. We need to distinguish between taking responsibility and self-blaming. It's very tempting to think: "If I am the creator of my life, and something bad happens, it's my fault." This kind of thinking is not helpful. Instead, you need to realize that everything in your life was created by you, but not everything was created by the conscious part of you. Everyone, including your past self, acts as consciously as he or she is able to act in the moment. In my experience, letting go of blame altogether is the single most effective practice that will change

---

15   Energy management' basically just means how you interact with the energies in your environment, specifically how you interact with other people.

your relationship to your reality. There is a vast difference between feeling anger, hurt or fear and blaming someone because you feel anger, hurt or fear. When we blame others, we drop into victim consciousness, and that simply doesn't support us. Whenever we blame someone, no matter how justified the blame is, we leak energy. The practice of not blaming other people is for your own benefit more than theirs.

Let's use a practical example: Imagine that someone abused you in the past, and you felt victimized. Of course there will be emotions of anger and grief. These wounded aspects easily go into the pattern of telling stories and assigning blame. Whether it is blaming oneself for allowing the abuse, or blaming the abuser or blaming life, these aspects are tangled in mental explanations. What we can do instead of getting caught in these stories of the mind, is to focus on and feel the physical sensation of the emotion. If the emotion is anger or rage, we can let ourselves feel that instinctive, animalistic feeling, and we can express it in a safe space. For example, we can let the rage out through the voice, through shaking the body, through punching a pillow or through crying. In this way, we can face the emotion directly, and accept it, without losing energy on blame. Moreover, blame is a defence mechanism, a tool we use to escape feeling very uncomfortable emotions, such as shame. Letting go of blame strengthens our true self-worth. Naturally, low self-worth will keep us from stepping fully into our creator nature.

2. *Take care of your boundaries*. The previous point adressed dealing with past experiences. As conscious creators, we also need to face challenging situations in the now-moment and be prepared to respond to them in a conscious way. Of course,

the most important thing is to be present, because one can only be conscious to the extent that one is present. When it comes to relationships and interactions with other people, a lot of creating your reality comes from knowing your boundaries, and expressing them. Boundaries change from moment to moment, so it's a matter of continuously tuning in with yourself. By boundaries, I don't mean putting energetic walls between you and another person, or being cold and distant. What I mean by boundaries is clearly choosing and expressing what you accept or don't accept in a given situation. It can be as simple as saying: "Hey, when you said that, I felt hurt." Or: "That doesn't feel good to me. Let's try to find another alternative". Or: "I don't know why I'm feeling this, but since you did that action today, I felt this tightness in my stomach. I think my pain-body is being triggered." Voicing our feelings and needs is the most important factor in setting healthy boundaries.

Obviously you can't command another person to do something (if you want to be sovereign and treat others as sovereign beings as well). But what you can do is to express or even declare, in a respectful way, how you want to be treated by another person. When you have a need that involves someone else, it is your responsibility to find that person who is willing to provide you with that need, to communicate that need to him or her and to allow yourself to receive the meeting of that need. As a master, it is your responsibility to address your self-worth issues so that you are able to receive love. At the same time, allowing yourself to receive unconditional love or acceptance will heal those self-worth issues. It is your responsibility to say, "No, I don't accept this", when someone crosses your boundaries, and your responsibility to leave a relationship that is imbalanced despite your best efforts to save the relationship. The more our boundaries have been dismissed in the past, the harder it is for us to respect our own boundaries. But it is so worth it! Practice communicating your boundaries to conscious people in your life, and you will gradually learn to place your boundaries in other situations as well.

3.   *Know what you like and express your desires.* Especially when it comes to relationships, this is essential. You can tell another person how you would like the situation to unfold, instead of telling him or her what you don't like. Rather than blaming or criticizing another's behaviour, you can say: "I would like to be treated this way from now on." Or you can say: "For me it is important that you call me and let me know if you're going to be 15 minutes late". Or: "Today I need a lot of physical affection, so if you can hug me and kiss me throughout the day, I'd be grateful". The more concrete, clear and specific you are in your expression of needs and desires, the easier it is for the other person to meet them in a concrete way. We often assume that the people around us know what we need and want, and then we take it as a personal insult if they don't respect those needs and desires. In many cases, however, they don't know, or they forgot, and all that is needed is for you to continuously and *consciously communicate* what is important for you. It is also very helpful to thank them and acknowledge when the other person treats you the way you would like to be treated. Communication really is magic in this world.

4.   *Walk away from that which doesn't serve you.* There are also certain situations, where no matter what you do or say, the other person keeps treating you in a less than respectful way. If nothing else has worked, blaming them will not work

either. Sometimes the best thing you can do is to simply *walk away* from the situation. This can mean walking away from a relationship that doesn't evolve despite your conscious choices, but it can also mean walking away from a conversation, a party, a job, and so on... This applies to any situation where you find yourself in but can't accept. If you can't accept the situation and you can't change it either, then walk away. As you can see, being a master doesn't require mastery of quantum physics; what it does require is heaps of compassion for self and others, authenticity and the courage to allow change.

5.   *Don't be scared of resistance or obstacles.* Obstacles often interfere with conscious creatorship because of unconscious or supressed needs and desires that contradict with our conscious desires, as mentioned before. Even though on a conscious level we are committed to our enlightenment, there are still very human aspects within us with human needs, desires and emotions. These aspects, when they are ignored, are like anchors keeping us stuck in old patterns.

There are different schools of thought regarding how to make sure that our humanity doesn't stand in the way of our divinity. For example, the Zen-approach teaches pure presence, and the idea is that intense presence will burn away any false emotions, thoughts, needs or desires until only our pure consciousness remains. This might be an effective approach if one is living excluded in a monastery. However, my experience is that for someone living within society and facing less conscious people on a daily basis, that approach is really hard. A more modern approach is to integrate the human with the divine self. This doesn't mean that our human personality will remain untouched; of course it will go through a profound transfiguration. But unlike many of the traditional approaches to enlightenment, the new one isn't about "starving off the ego" or about giving up our humanity. Instead we are infusing the human identity with so much consciousness that it naturally transforms. This new approach is about loving and accepting every part of our human self, including every desire, need and emotion that we feel. It doesn't mean that we try to satisfy each desire that we feel. But we acknowledge each desire and go deep enough to ask what the real issue is. Often desires are masking a deeper need within us, and only through awareness can we integrate the core issue. Most of these human needs and desires evaporate simply by us allowing them, by breathing deeply and feeling our emotions without judgment, and loving ourselves unconditionally in every moment. If we still have an unmet need after that, it will become very clear to us what we need to do.

Whenever we feel resistance, we know that there is an aspect within us pulling us in the opposite direction. Instead of trying to force the resistance to change, you can breathe with it, accept it and love yourself unconditionally while you are feeling the resistance. Once all parts of you, human aspects and divine self, are aligned in divine will, conscious creation becomes very easy. This is a dynamic, on-going process of constantly breathing with any resistance that shows up and returning back to the alignment of Self, again and again. Instead of seeing obstacles as evidence of your inability to create consciously, you can perceive obstacles as an inevitable, boring and fairly harmless part of human life.

6.   *Release expectations and don't try to control the outcome.* A very important factor of conscious creating is to release all

attachments to your creations: This means releasing the agenda and the expectations about how and when the creation will unfold, and what the result will be. On a practical level, a conscious creator might have a clear intention and make an initial plan, but also allow a flexibility to change direction when necessary and allow a space for unexpected results. Again, it's about applying the AND consciousness: For example, if you have a dream, you can accept your current situation as it is, and practice getting really comfortable in the present moment. And, at the same time, you can take active, effortless steps in the direction of your joy – without being attached to when or how your dream will be fulfilled. It's about enjoying the process of dreaming and each step of the progress as much as arriving at the fulfilment of the dream. You can perceive creations as flowers: They bloom when they are ready to bloom, not when you want them to; you are here to witness the miracle of the unfolding flower.

7.   *Let go of force.* I guarantee, it's possible to create miracles without effort and hard work; you don't need to force or push energies for them to move! Energies move easily when you act with joy, ease and grace. When you act from a place of inspiration, rather than a place of trying to manipulate and control energies, creativity flows in abundance, and support shows up easily, and the creation flows down-river rather than against the stream. You might have noticed that I have not mentioned affirmations, positive thinking, and other tools that most teachers of conscious manifestation offer. First of all, I believe there is no shortage of such information, which is why I'm not repeating it here. More importantly, what has worked for me was not to use tools to manifest something specific in my life, but rather to address the parts within me that were

pressing the breaks, so to speak. Conscious manifesting is effortless; it's an act of allowing the creation to emerge. Effort only attracts more effort. That is why the focus here is not on how to move forward, but rather on how to get out of the way of your inherent, natural creative flow. You don't need to create the creative flow; you only need to undo the dam and flow downstream.

8. *Be proud of your creations and grateful for what you have now*. This might be a cliché, but it's a helpful cliché. The more we allow ourselves to notice, receive and appreciate the gifts that come our way, the easier it will be to create more beauty, abundance and love in our life. It's not about pretending to be grateful when we are really depressed, but rather about being present in this moment and, in an authentic way, noticing the small things that we like about this particular moment.

Now that we have discussed some of the principles of conscious creatorship, we can take a look at the other attributes of sovereignty.

The Sovereign Domain

You don't become a sovereign, free being – you always have been one. You just become aware of being one; the transformation that is happening is nothing more than a divine creator awakening into remembrance of his inherent freedom and creatorship after lifetimes of illusion. Your powers of creatorship are so real that you created an entire reality to serve your belief of being small and limited. What's the point, one might ask. Consider that the only way to truly understand creatorship is through experiencing the contrast, which is powerlessness. You created a veil, allowed yourself to forget, and you even forgot that there was something to forget in the first place. You didn't just create a theatre on Earth. Your created such a real stage that your incarnations, the enacted roles, forgot that they were actors. Self-realization is the choice to remember that inherent sovereignty while being on this stage called Earth and to embody this sovereignty through the human form.

So what does claiming your sovereignty mean in practical terms?

1.   Taking responsibility for all of your creations, without blaming yourself or judging your creations, as discussed previously. If you don't like the word 'responsibility', replace it with 'owning your freedom': Acknowledge and own the fact that you are free to create and choose the life you want to live.

2.   Choosing what serves you in the now moment and releasing everything that doesn't serve you. Sometimes we are not clear about what we truly want, because the human fears and layers of conditioning are hiding our true desires; what we think we should want or what we want to want may be covering what we really want. But that's the beautiful thing about life: each choice that we make reveals us more about what actually serves us. What serves us might occasionally feel scary or uncomfortable, but it also brings a sense of relief, relaxation, expansion, spaciousness, inner peace or joy. These are all signs of you going into a direction that is in alignment with your inner master. Whether it's a relationship or a diet or a life choice that you're unsure about, listen to your body's

sensations, because they express the unconscious feelings that are filtered by the analytic mind. For instance, ask yourself, how do I feel about choosing scenario 1? And then listen to the instinctive physical sensations. Repeat with the other options, and compare to see which option feels most expansive.

3.   Deriving energy from your sovereign source. We are used to taking and receiving energy in very particular patterns, and most of them involve imbalanced transaction or energy exchange between others and ourselves. However, when you realize your inherent sovereignty, you realize that you don't need to take energy from outside of yourself. We are used to getting energy from food, light, water and air. On a cellular level, our DNA is also transforming and we are moving into a new system where we don't need to get our energy from outside ourselves. However, this is a natural process that we can't influence too much and that might take a long time to unfold.

What is more relevant for us to discuss here is deriving emotional or psychic energy. For example, love, connection and passion are very important to us as humans, since we are a social species. We have learned to exchange emotional energy with our fellow humans in ways that are usually not balanced or healthy. We generally treat interactions like transactions: "You give me this much love and I give you this much back." In sovereignty, you are consciously connected to your soul, which is an unlimited source of love, passion and belongingness. When you consciously view your relationships as *expressions* of love, rather than the source of love, the way of exchanging energy changes drastically. It will transform from a type of transaction into an unconditional giving and receiving. This doesn't mean that you stop receiving outside energies; the difference is that instead of manipulating circumstances to get energy, you concentrate on your soul-connection, your personal source of unlimited love. This gives you the opportunity to interact with others as they are, without an agenda to change them or to get something from them. It means that you receive energy without holding on to it and you give energy without holding back. You transform from being a hunter of energy to a channel that allows energies to come and go freely. You might still have human needs for connection and intimacy, but you realize that self-love is the basis upon which you can build loving relationships with others.

As a sovereign master, you are so centred in your self-trust that you naturally attract the energies that are needed in the moment. This natural, energy-abundant state is only possible once you let go of the need to have power, which is a human-created substitute for the natural free flow of energy. This requires your unflinching trust in your own inherent ability to attract whatever you need, without assuming that your ego-self knows what you actually need. Self-trust becomes stronger through practice, and while you are in the process of returning to your natural self-trust, allow yourself to receive help from others. Unconditional receiving is as much a part of sovereignty as unconditional giving, and for many of us, it is more pattern-breaking and thus challenging.

4.   Living in mastery also means becoming aware of your multidimensional nature. Yes, you are embodied as a human and have a human personality, but you become aware of the other dimensions of yourself, the other identities and expressions of your soul. In mastery, you don't restrict yourself

to being only one identity. For example, in dream-state we are often completely different to our waking-state identity, yet it's still a real aspect of us.

5.   As a sovereign being, you approach problems very differently than most humans do. Mastery isn't about never having a problem again, never falling down or getting lost; a master can get totally lost, because he always finds his way back to his core. There is no such thing as a perfect human, but there is a divine human – YOU. In sovereignty, there will still be problems, but they don't drain your energy. As a master, you focus less on problems, because they become less interesting than other aspects of your life. You will start to notice that problems tend to solve themselves; you know that they will be resolved somehow without you having to put effort into them. It's possible to take action without putting effort into it! As a matter of fact, problems get resolved much more gracefully when you stop worrying about them and simply trust and choose that they will resolve themselves, while you return your focus to the present moment. Yes, problems come and go, and will continue to do so, but your life doesn't revolve around them anymore.

6.   The question we undoubtedly come to face in our quest for sovereignty is what freedom really means. Freedom from what and whom? Does freedom mean we become reckless rebels? Yes and no. When you claim your sovereignty in a world that is built on limitation, control and fear, it can appear reckless or rebellious. Here is my view on freedom:

As small children, we see our parents as Gods. This is understandable, given that we came into this life through our mother's womb, and were dependent on our primary caregivers for survival. We knew that in order to survive, we had to maintain a pleasing relationship to them. This is the origin of authority figures in our lives. As we grew older and started to understand more about this world, we also realized that our parents are not all-powerful, all-knowing and all perfect; they make mistakes, too. And so the illusion of their authority started to crack, and by the time we reached adolescence, we were learning that not only are we separate from our parents, but we are also independent of them. We realized that their authority is based on our respect. Similarly, as we awaken, we start to question the authority figures in our life, whether it's our boss or the government, our own limiting beliefs or something else.

Unlike our teenage-self, however, we don't need to rebel *against* the system. We can simply expand *beyond* it; we can acknowledge that to be part of society, we must accept certain rules of the system, but at the same time we acknowledge that this is not our whole reality. We might still abide the laws, but we do this willingly and consciously because we choose to be part of society. What changes is our perception of and relationship to power: We step out of the world of power, because we can see that it is nothing more than a game of duality. We step out of the power-matrix not in order to change it, but because we know that there are other, more natural ways of attaining energy. When we step out of the power-dynamic, then the emotional charge in our interactions dissolves. In practical terms this could mean, for example, that we still go to work and respect the leadership of the employer, but we don't see them as an authority figure; we see them as a being of consciousness. We don't see ourselves as part of a hierarchy;

instead work becomes a neutral, temporary role that we choose to play for as long as it feels appropriate. Freedom means we allow ourselves to be who we are, but we also allow others to be who they are.

7.   Sovereignty also means freedom from the illusion of time; as a master, you move beyond time and space. While this might sound metaphysical, it's also common sense. In the same way that your life doesn't revolve around problems anymore, your choices aren't made by the hypnotic suggestions of mass consciousness and your identity isn't limited to your human persona, similarly, gravity is no longer the force that balances you when you choose mastery. *What grounds you doesn't have to be gravity and what determines the rhythm of your life, doesn't have to be time.* When you become centred in yourself, time and space move through you. They always have, but in that moment you realize the illusion of linearity. In other words, your consciousness is and always has been the sun around which your reality revolves, but now you have the awareness to see that. You are not a helpless fish caught in the net of time and space; you are the conductor of the symphony of your reality, and time/space are your instruments. Instead of seeing yourself as the servant of the clock, you can allow time to serve you.

This applies to everything else as well, including the people and the situations in your life: As a master, you allow energies to serve you. The truth is that energies always have served you, but the moment that you consciously realize this, they start serving you in a more graceful way, because they reflect your radiance – if you radiate self-doubt and victim-consciousness, the energies will treat you like a victim; radiate mastery, and the energies will treat you like a master.

8.   Perhaps the essence of sovereignty is the simple realization that "I exist". I exist *no matter what*. I may die, I may break my heart, I may experience hell but I still exist. This realization, which really is the core of mastery, will open the door to many more epiphanies. Once you realize that you exist as an eternal, souled being, a sovereign being whose existence is independent of anyone and anything, you will also become a lot more independent in your human life. And I don't mean independent in terms of finances, or knowing how to fix your car, I mean spiritually and intellectually independent. You stop needing the advice and opinions of other people, because now you are connected to your own intuition, and other people's opinions become a lot less relevant. In other words, you stop living your life for other people, and start living for yourself. Don't feel sorry for them – they have their own life to live for themselves.

9.   Sovereignty is about reclaiming yourself. It's an *attitude* of independence. It's the realization that "I'm not here to perform life, to entertain others, to please my parents, to perfect my children, to compete against anyone, to perform well in school, or at work or anywhere else. I own my life. I'm here to experience life as ME, and that 'me' is whatever I choose in the moment, and it can change. I don't live to survive, to enhance my ego, to avoid mistakes, to feel guilty about what I'm not or ashamed about what I am, to run away from death or to justify my existence. I am here, with this consciousness, in this body, on this Earth to experience, express and expand the conscious creator that I am!" … In the end, your sovereignty truly is yours – nobody can take it from you or give it to you, other than yourself. The title of a 'master' is one that can only be bestowed or withdrawn by the Self; that's what makes it sovereign.

Sovereignty ≠ Isolation

Sovereignty doesn't mean that you have to isolate yourself, and disconnecting from your past/your limitations doesn't mean you have to disconnect from other people; it simply means you connect to others from a place of freedom, rather than a place of transaction. It means that you connect so deeply to yourself, that you can now in fact connect with other people on a much deeper and more authentic level. When you are no longer afraid of your own darkness, then you stop being afraid of other people. When you know who you are, you can allow yourself to "meld" with another person, to dive into their energies and allow them to come really close to you without worrying about losing yourself. Being sovereign doesn't mean that you shouldn't need or want anything from other people! Rather, it's about acknowledging your own needs and at the same time acknowledging that nobody owes you anything, because you are the creator of your life and other people are the creators of their lives.

Sovereignty just means that you no longer live in fear of powerlessness, because you don't depend on power. In sovereignty you are not attached to other people, because you are not attached to the power given to you by others. Once you go beyond fear, power has no power over you and this changes the dynamics of interaction. Instead of being attached to other people, you can experience authenticity, intimacy and closeness with others in a safe space. And you don't have to disconnect from society either; you can still use money, work in a company and buy your vegetables at the supermarket as a sovereign being. The difference is that you don't take these actions from a perception of limitation, but from a perception of freedom and choice. The most important shift that takes place as you transition into sovereignty is how you see yourself: As a limited human who needs to fight for survival or as a conscious creator who is here to create and enjoy experiences.

To Be or Not To Be Employed … or How to Make a Conscious Choice

~ *Your choices don't define who you are; they simply define your experience.* ~

Related to the subject of freedom and sovereignty is the business of making choices. As we awaken, our choices change drastically. Not only do our priorities change, but also the process that we use to make a choice. Many people on the spiritual path struggle with making choices in their human life, such as whether to stay in a job or leave, whether to study, whether to be self-employed instead... I certainly have struggled with it! If you find yourself in this situation, know that it doesn't matter too much what you are currently doing. You are worthy of life no matter what job you do or don't do. Your enlightenment will unfold if you have chosen it no matter how you create money to fund your living.

You don't need to choose one profession, one identity or one label – you can integrate all your facets into your current activity. Nobody really cares about what you do, others care about what you are because people hope to see a standard, a living example of someone who is fully here, fully engaged and participating in life with their whole heart and soul. It doesn't matter whether you are serving coffee or creating world peace, what matters is that you pour all of yourself into your doings. (By the way, if you truly want to save the world or even make it a slightly better place, start with yourself – it's arrogant to try to change your surroundings if you're not prepared to change yourself.) And as for purpose, who says you need to have *a* purpose in life? Have as many purposes as you like. If you're not sure what your purpose is, start by letting go of everything that doesn't feel meaningful or joyful. Let go of things that really don't matter and are draining your energy – walking away from people and situations that you know are not in alignment with you is one of the best things you can do in terms of self-love and grace-allowing. It also creates space for opportunities and people that are in alignment with you, even if you don't know what and who those are. It's really as simple as being fully present in whatever you are doing, and if you still object to the activity/situation/person involved in it, take it as a sign that it's time to make changes.

Please know and acknowledge that every choice that you have made in the past was the best choice you could make at the time with the knowledge and resources that were available to you at the time – otherwise you wouldn't have made it. Perhaps you can't go back into the past to change the actual events that took place, but you can heal the past by looking at what happened from a more expanded, compassionate and self-loving perspective. The important thing is that your choices, even if you or other people have judged them as wrong, have brought you where you are today: To a place of priceless experience, wisdom and self-knowledge.

If you are facing a crossroad, it's always beneficial to *feel* into the options rather than think about them: How does your body feel when you imagine yourself choosing one of the options? How does your heart and chest feel? How do you feel energetically? Does your body respond differently to the other option? Do you feel a general lightness or heaviness regarding either option? Do you feel expanded or constricted? These sensations are clues as to what is most in alignment with you. Keep it simple, be authentic with yourself and trust what you feel.

If, after this experiment, you still feel unclear, you can always go for 'trial and error'. However, instead of plunging headfirst into a direction that you're not completely sure of, it might be more self-loving to gently take a few steps into one direction, and then observe how it feels. Usually when we go against our natural flow of ease and grace, against our alignment, we quickly notice feelings such as stagnation, heaviness, exhaustion, anxiety, etc. On the other hand, if we're going in the direction that is in alignment with our soul, life generally flows in a more fluent, synchronous or joyful way. Resistance and fear will still be present until we have integrated them, so don't treat them as directives to change direction. In alignment, we will still face obstacles now and then, but in general, there will be a feeling of 'being in tune' with ourselves. Remember that feeling of having butterflies in the belly: That sweet tingle that feels invigorating and exciting, and at the same time makes you feel completely nervous. This is the kind of sensation that is typical when we choose something that is in alignment with soul, but outside of our comfort zone.

Remember that you always have the freedom to change your mind, your desires or your direction, because change is the essence of growth and expansion. Sometimes you can't undo an old choice, but you can always make a new choice regarding your now-moment.

In addition to making a decision when you're at a crossroad, you can also make 'conscious choices'. A conscious choice is more like an announcement that you, as the conscious creator of your life, make to the universe and to yourself. You can make a conscious choice before seeing the various options available to you, because you have a deep understanding that you can create the options that you need. You can make a conscious choice without seeing, planning or knowing how your choice will be realized! Whereas a decision is based on choosing the better option available to you, a conscious choice is limitless. Instead of choosing the better option, you choose the best option without worrying about 'how' or when you will get there.

Another aspect of making a conscious choice is that you don't need to know the details. For example, you can make a choice to create/attract a work position that fulfils the characteristics and the qualities that you desire without having to know which profession or which company can provide that for you. Instead you simply make the choice and trust that your inner master and your creative essence will manifest your dream job (or partner or house) for you in the appropriate way at the appropriate time. Once you've made the choice, set it free and release all expectations, trusting that it will eventually return to you in the form of a beautiful creation.

You can also make conscious choices that are more general, such as:

I am done with suffering.
I am done with blaming my past.
I am done with trying to fix myself.
I am done with effort.
I am done with lying to myself.
I am done with judging myself.
I am done with letting problems define my experience.

I choose to live.
I choose to be grounded and present in my body.
I choose a safe space in all areas of my life.
I choose abundance.
I choose to receive love.
I choose to perceive life through the eyes of my inner master.
I choose my enlightenment.

It might sound simplistic to make such a general choice, but the clearer you are about your choices, the easier it is for those choices to manifest. I also love to use my actual voice to state my conscious choices – partly to inform the universe to support me and partly to remind myself that I am the creator of my life.

The Magic of Allowing

~ One of the simple secrets of living in mastery is that you don't have to step on the gas – you just need to take your foot off the breaks. ~

Have you noticed my frequent use of the word "allowing" in

this book? This is because allowing is not only the definition of graceful living and mastery, but it's also the most important step in realizing your enlightenment. Allowing means letting the energies flow, letting go of resisting whatever is, and realizing that energies are always in your service. It means giving up the fight against yourself. When I talk about allowing, I'm not referring to outside forces, such as allowing other people to abuse you; 'allowing', as used here, is an internal act. Allowing means letting yourself be all of who you are; instead of fearing your own darkness or your own brightness (or both), you can invite all of yourself to flow through you. It's letting the feelings come and letting the feelings go. Allowing means trusting that whatever is yours will integrate, and whatever is not will drop away, and trusting that whatever you need will come to you in the right way at the right time. It means not holding on to anything except your true Self. Embodied enlightenment means allowing
your divinity to be present in this reality. Allowing is your natural state of being and the prerequisite for living an authentically joyful life.

What does allowing look like in practical terms? Let's say, something happened today that triggered you, and now you feel angry. You take a deep breath, all the way to your belly, and you allow yourself to really *feel* the anger. Do this in a safe space – by yourself or in the company of someone who can stay present with you despite the energies of anger. Allow the feelings to flow through you without resistance and, at the same time, also allow yourself to perceive the situation through the eyes of your inner master. Continue breathing and letting the energies flow until you feel them naturally rebalance. That's it! The more you practice this, the more trust you will have in the process.

Allowing also means radiating your light without holding back. Instead of hiding your beauty, creativity and uniqueness, you can allow yourself and other people to see and to hear you. Allowing starts when we start to forgive ourselves for everything there is to forgive and eventually realize that there wasn't anything to forgive in the first place. The more fully we allow self-forgiveness to sink into our hearts and bodies, the more we start to trust our essence, and then allowing happens naturally.

Allowing is like being a channel for your own soul: Imagine being in a constant state of receiving the infinite love that soul has for you, while continuously releasing anything and everything that no longer serves you. Allowing happens when life becomes more important to you than fear, when you prioritize self-acceptance above appearing like a 'good citizen'. You will probably still feel fear in mastery, but you no longer let it come between you and your divinity. Another way of describing allowing is taking down the filters, the censorship, and the walls that you have placed between the different parts of yourself – like pulling open the heavy curtains between your conscious and your subconscious aspects. Allowing is the cornerstone of mastery and the secret to creating in the new energy, which brings us to the last chapter of living in mastery.

New Energy – New Earth

With every change of perspective, our reality changes also. Once we have mastered our own aspects and released our past, we are ready to play with new energy and our inherent multi-dimensional nature. To clear one common misunderstanding, having extrasensory abilities is *not* the measure of how awakened a person is, or how committed to his enlightenment. One can be very conscious without having the ability to see or hear other-dimensional beings, for example. However, individuals who are awakening often become curious about the dimensions beyond this physical reality, which is why I have discussed some safe ways of exploring these dimensions. Sometimes it also happens that an awakening human spontaneously opens her third eye, but this is not always the case. Just understand that being able to see auras or hear angels has nothing to do with your enlightenment, although it might make your journey more interesting. It is possible to bring the magic back into life without being clairvoyant; magic is a perspective of reality.

Stepping Into a Multi-Dimensional Perspective

Dimensions aren't hierarchical levels or places that you achieve, nor do you have to 'travel' to them; they are simply different ways of perceiving and experiencing reality. If you are wondering how you can see, feel and experience the various layers of your existence, in other words, bring the magic back into your reality, then here are some helpful tools to get you started:

1. Dreams

The purpose of dreams is to allow us to get a break from the density of mass consciousness and to reconnect with our source consciousness. Dreams can provide important messages from your intuition about things that require your attention, or about future potentials that you may have overlooked. They provide an opportunity for your mind to rest, your creativity to flow freely, your body to rejuvenate and your subconscious aspects to rise to the surface. Our waking state is becoming increasingly mental, to the extent that we have difficulty having actual felt experiences, because we are too busy intellectualizing everything and living life from one mental construct to the next. Dreams provide an opportunity to mentally "lose control" in a way that doesn't harm the human self.

Everybody dreams at night, but not everyone remembers his or her dreams. You can easily train yourself to remember your dreams by starting a dream journal: Place some paper and a pen beside your bed. Before you go to sleep, make a conscious choice to remember your dreams in the morning. Make sure your alarm clock isn't too loud or disturbing. Ideally you want to slowly slide from your dreaming-state into your waking state. When you wake up, try to lie completely still and keep your eyes closed, and go through any remembrances of dreams. Perhaps you can only remember one detail or a vague feeling. Write it down. If you remember a whole scenario, go through the entire sequence of events several times and then write it down. Ask your intuition what this dream is telling you. Not all dreams are significant, but every once in a while, you can have a life-altering dream. The more you pay attention to your dreams, the more they start coming into your consciousness.

I've had some of my most enlightening experiences in my dream-state. Dreams also tend to become more intense as we awaken and integrate our aspects; this is nothing to be afraid of – in fact, most of the shadow figures that appear in dreams are our own aspects. As for the rest, they can only reach you through your fear, and once fear is released, no dark astral beings can reach you.

2. Symbolism

Life is symbolic. The macrocosm is reflected through the microcosm, the spiritual is reflected through the material, and so forth. Symbols help us to perceive the wider perspective, the big picture. Symbols are the language of the intuition. When you open up to the magic of life itself, and allow yourself to be playful, you will notice the intricate web of communication and connection that curses through life. Symbols are the messengers between this dimension and other dimensions. Your life has an undercurrent stream of atmosphere, much like a movie has a soundtrack that casts a certain mood and atmosphere over the scene. This atmosphere reveals itself through the synchronous dance of little details. Have you noticed how days that turn out to bear great significance in your life, are preceded by subtle hints of the upcoming twist of fate? This dance of synchronicity is often presented to us through symbols. Symbols are universal *and* highly personal, and can be either concrete or more abstract. Almost anything can become a symbol under the right circumstances, and its significance depends on its relation and meaning to you. If you find yourself constantly and unusually surrounded by a particular animal, or repeatedly hearing a particular song, you could ask yourself what this animal or song means for you? If a particular colour appears vividly in your dream, ask what this colour symbolizes.

Paying attention to symbols is also a way of inviting playfulness and creativity into your life. You can also create new symbols, or give new meanings to old symbols. For example, a wedding band doesn't have to symbolize that you are 'bound' to your spouse for the rest of your lifetime, unless you want it to symbolize that. You could give it a new meaning, such as being a token of the openhearted, respectful commitment between you and your partner for as long as the relationship serves both of you.

Symbols also reveal much about our shadow aspects. For example, think of a symbol that you would use to represent motherhood. What is the first image that pops into your mind? This gives you an idea about the subconscious relationship you have with your own mother. Another way how you can use symbols to get in touch with hidden aspects is to write a fairy tale, or a poem: you will notice that without consciously trying to do so, your creative writing will be filled with symbolism that reveals much about your aspects. The same applies to any creative expression, such as painting or dramatic improvisation.

3. **Synchronicity**

Symbols are an expression of synchronicity, which is the natural flow of things. Life is always synchronous, but we can choose to either be aware of it or not. Synchronicity appears when we expand our perspective to see the interconnectedness of seemingly disconnected parts of life. Ask yourself: Is there a specific theme in your current life that appears to you wherever you look? What draws your attention; what attracts you; what is the current rhythm, melody, mood or story running through your life?

A great exercise in synchronicity is to start noticing abundance in all areas of your life. Soon enough you will discover that the more attention you pay to abundance (forgive the pun), the more it shows up in your life. It doesn't matter whether it shows up because you pay attention to it or whether it only becomes more apparent as you notice it. The point is that you can allow synchronicity to serve your perspective of lack, or your perspective of abundance. You can deliberately focus on things that make you feel joyful, such as beauty, art, design, nature and so on. Your point of focus will then start attracting that specific vibration into your life. Acknowledging the synchronicities of life is an invitation for your magical self to become more present in your life. Once you start becoming more adept at noticing synchronicity, it will also become easier to trust your own manifestation abilities. Synchronicity is the manifestation of the 'law of attraction', which means that your external reality mirrors your internal reality: The more you start noticing and paying attention to magic, beauty, love, joy and abundance, the more these things will be present in your life. Your perception has influence over that which is perceived, as quantum scientists are discovering; your perspective creates realities, in other words.

4.   Inner Space

It is very easy to get lost in the mentally driven matrix of mass consciousness. You'll know that you are entangled in its lucrative web when you feel a constant, frenzied need to do something; you have become addicted to nervousness, stress and adrenaline. Even if you consciously try to relax, you can't. When you don't feel your passion for life, when your creativity is suffocated, and life just doesn't feel like the sensual, thrilling experience that it really is. Sadly, this state of being (or rather, doing) is what we have come to accept as the norm. This obsession with thinking life rather than living it restricts our ability to be aware of other dimensions.

If this is the case, it's time to disconnect from the outside world and to re-connect with your inner world. Even if this is not the case, connecting to our inner self is always a good idea. There are countless dimensions within you, and many ways to connect with your inner space. Here are some of my favourites:

• Feeling your *Body of Consciousness*: You start by taking a few deep, sensual breaths. While breathing deeply, feel your physical body, from the outside by caressing yourself, and from within by becoming aware of any sensations in the body. Then feel your consciousness present in the body, feel your life force energy alive and flowing through every cell in your body. Acknowledge that you are a physical being *and* an eternal being. Become aware of being a channel for your divinity, your soul.

• Journaling: Write about your current feeling-state and about anything that feels relevant. Write what your aspects are feeling, and also write with the voice of your wisdom/ soul. Writing about your experiences allows you to observe them and thus create a "breathing space" between yourself and your aspects. The purpose of this is to feel your emotions and yet see through their illusion. When you journal just for yourself, you consciously connect with yourself. It's like having a conversation that allows your aspects to express their feelings, and it also allows you to hear your soul-voice more clearly. You might even be surprised by the wisdom of your soul.

• Meditation and *Dreamwalking*: 'Dreamwalking' means consciously "travelling" into non-physical dimensions. Naturally, in non-physical dimensions time and space are irrelevant, so 'travelling' here is more of a metaphor. For example, you can create an inner sanctuary in your meditation. You might call this mere imagination, but have you considered that in some other dimensions, which do not operate in time and space, imagination could appear as more real of an experience than material reality? For instance, I've had dreams that felt more real than this reality, despite being less physical...

Dreamwalking is also a good way to connect with lost aspects of ourselves. You can literally dreamwalk yourself into the history of your "past" lifetimes. Remembering other incarnations of one's soul can also become a distraction rather than a tool to our awakening. Because we are multi-dimensional beings, we don't need to leave our bodies to travel somewhere with our consciousness (as is typically the case with 'astral travel'). It's usually much safer and just as efficient to dreamwalk while being consciously grounded in the physical body. This type of meditation is one where instead of leaving your physical consciousness, you *expand* beyond it. For example, you could do a dreamwalk to meet your future self.

• Being instead of doing: The concept of being in a state of 'not doing' is quite popular in spiritual literature for a reason. It's extremely simple, and very difficult if you are not used to it. Try sitting on a couch for fifteen minutes by yourself, in silence, without doing anything. Not even meditating, not listening to music, but just feeling yourself, enjoying your own company. Unless you are practiced at this kind of thing, chances are your mind will become very loud. Emotions might come to the surface. You might hear aspects shouting that you need to do something productive instead of sitting here doing nothing; the world might fall apart if you just sit in complete stillness, the mind says. The harder this non-doing feels, the more disconnected you are from your inner dimensions. The tricky thing is that you can't force the state of being – the moment it turns into a discipline, you are again trying to accomplish something, which means you are again escaping the opportunity to just be with yourself unconditionally. With time, this state of nothingness can bring you face to face with your divinity. Truly, the most interesting dimensions are not somewhere out there in space, but right here within the spaciousness of ourselves.

5. Imagination

Imagination is such an important quality and gift that we possess, and too often forget about as adults. Imagination opens up the mind to new ideas, to different dimensions of the Self and it even helps to keep us mentally balanced. There are no rules when it comes to using the imagination. The point of imagination is to let go of mental control and to let your creativity roam freely. Instead of doing forceful visualizations where you direct your visual focus, let the imagination direct itself. Otherwise it's just another mind-control technique; you can't transcend your mind using mental strategies such as control. Control is the mind's attept to navigate reality, and therefore the only way to go beyond the mind is to let go of control, forced concentration and efforting, and instead allow the imagination to *flow* without inhibition.

Allow feelings to flow into the mind, and you will experience sensual imagination. Imagine with all of your senses, not just with your visual sense. Imagine with an open heart, with childish playfulness and outrageous, unbridled freedom. Imagine without goals, but simply for the fun of it. Imagine with a twist of humour, with pleasure and passion, imagine the possible and the impossible, the important and the silly things. Imagine with a twinkle in your eye and a hint of smile upon your lips. When you feel fear, imagine that fear-scenario with grotesque detail and dress it up with silliness. Imagination can also be used for manifestation purposes. Just because imagination doesn't obey the rules of the physical reality doesn't mean it's not real! It's simply a different dimension of reality – a dimension that can serve you, if you let it.

6. Going Beyond Time

When you expand your consciousness and become aware of different dimensions, your way of sensing time changes. This can benefit anyone who feels stressed chasing the clock, or daunted by the idea of life slipping through her fingers despite her best efforts to package it into schedules. We are literally running from one appointment to the other, and constantly learning to run faster, while at the same time trying to stop the passing of time in an anti-aging campaign – we are running towards death while resisting and fearing it. However, the fact is, you don't need to run. You don't need to run towards the future, or away from your past. Everything that matters is happening now because quantum-scientifically speaking, all times are contained within the now. For me it was surprising and delightful to discover that the now-moment is multi-dimensional; it's not just a narrow point of focus, but more like an expanded space of presence.

If you want to experiment with sensing time in a new way, you can do several things to shift your perspective on time:

• Whenever you think about the past, consciously anchor yourself in the present moment: Feel your body, ground yourself, remain aware of your surroundings, and breathe consciously while going into your memories. This will help to integrate your past into the present moment, and your energies won't be all scattered and fractured. The same applies when focusing on the future.

• Instead of just thinking about the past, feel into your memories. This will open your perception to a wider perspective. Allow yourself to *sensually feel* the many layers of sensation that you might have missed before. We tend to highlight our more dramatic memories and forget about beautiful, but more peaceful experiences – even though every experience happens on a multitude of levels, and is never just painful or dramatic. Whenever you go through an experience, it's not just one 'you' that is experiencing any given situation, but there are in fact countless aspects (in addition to your soul-essence) that are present.

When you perceive your memories more multi-dimensionally, your wounded self understands that there is a way out of the painful story. For example, if you visit a traumatic memory while consciously staying in your safe space in the expanded now-moment, you can become aware of your soul's presence during that traumatic event. Then your past self (that is kept alive by the unresolved pain in your subconscious) will realize that the situation wasn't all bad, but instead had many layers to it. It's like visiting your past self and bringing a souvenir (a new perspective) into that memory. This kind of inner work is extremely freeing, because it changes your relationship to your past.

• When you feel into future potentials, don't just think about them or visually see them with your mind's eye, but allow yourself to sensually feel them with all your senses, as well as with your heart. Ask soul to show you future potentials that are in alignment with your true desires. Don't expect visual images, although perhaps you will see them, but allow the intuition to flow in through whatever channel it chooses. Often our intuition uses symbols to communicate with us, not just in the outside world but also in our imagination and dream-state.

• Whenever you feel anxiety or stress regarding time pressures, take a deep breath and drop everything for a few minutes. Usually we get stressed because we feel that there are so many important things that need to be done right now, although we don't have the resources or capacity to do everything at once. Ask yourself: How important are these things really? One of the best things you can do in this kind of situation is to close your eyes, and see the big picture. Will these "very important things" be at all meaningful in five years' time? How important will these schedules be to you when you are lying on your deathbed? The point is, don't stress about things that are unimportant, and save you energy on things that truly matter to you – not on what other people say should matter to you... I call this the '*it-doesn't-matter*-technique'.

• Another short and simple exercise that you can do to relieve time-related stress is the following awareness-meditation: Close your eyes, take a deep breath, relax your shoulders, and start to notice any sounds that are surrounding you. Don't focus on any one particular sound, just let them come in and go out of your awareness. After a while of doing this, open your eyes and just notice whatever you are seeing without focusing on any particular point. Just observe your surroundings without analysing, naming, trying to understand or change them. Whenever your mind tries to draw your attention to some "important thoughts", gently redirect your relaxed attention to your environment – simply observing it. Realize that in this moment your only role is to observe your surroundings. This will bring you back into your beingness, and it will show you that the world doesn't fall apart the minute you stop focusing, controlling and rushing about. Afterwards you can return to your daily activities in a revitalized state and perhaps even learn how to hurry in a more relaxed manner. Or if you are really courageous, you might want to try living life without hurrying at all. Now that's mastery!

7. Sensuality

If you feel bored, depressed, drained or tired then it's likely that you've suppressed your sensuality and forgotten to feel life. Life is meant to be sensual and humans are highly sensual beings – there is a reason why we have a heart and consciousness; we are not robots (yet) and not meant to act like robots either. (This is not to say that there's anything wrong with going through depression.) Whenever you feel colourless, devote a moment to reawakening your senses. I don't mean just the physical senses, but all of your senses: Feel the energies of the day, of a place, a person or a situation. Allow yourself to feel subtle energies, as well as the raw, intense, physical energies. Sensuality can be sexual, but is not limited to it. It doesn't have to be directed outwards, but can be directed within – actually, being aware of your soul or feeling your self-love can be highly sensual experiences. Being sensual also means letting life and the energies you encounter soak into you, without fear that those energies might pollute you. It's a very open and even vulnerable state, but also very blissful. Allowing yourself to be sensual will make your life more colourful and vibrant.

Obviously, there are many other ways to explore multi-dimensionality, such as using the popular *Ayahuasca* drug, but in my experience any technique that is artificially induced does not serve our enlightenment: Although these kinds of medicines can momentarily open up our consciousness, they will not help us to integrate the new awareness into our lives. And embodied enlightenment is all about integrating consciousness into our human experiences. *Ayahuasca* may be a natural drug that can change your perspective and provide you with a thrilling experience, but it's not the most natural – or even the fastest – way to enlightenment. If in doubt, read *the Red Lion*. As always, you know best what serves you.

The Quantum Attributes of New Energy

~ New energy is free energy. It is not here to replace old energy, but to exist in parallel to it, as an alternative. ~

What comes after the New Age? The age of consciousness. We are experiencing transformation on various levels simultaneously: As an awakening human, you experience personal spiritual expansion, which means that you eventually move from operating in the old energy of duality, to operating in the old energy *and* the new energy. New energy in this context means creating and interacting with energies from a place of wisdom. The attributes of new energy are very quantum in their nature. The new energy is a way of describing a new way of creating reality that is not based on the old energetic laws, such as physical laws of probability or the effect of ancestral DNA, or spiritual laws such karma, life contracts, etc. The new law is based solely on freedom, and it is so pure, so refined that it will only become tangible to someone who is truly ready to expand beyond a power-based reality.

'Energy' here is defined as any form, expression or creation of consciousness, including all the physical elements of this universe, but also the non-physical forms. Every souled being is pure consciousness at its core, but in order to experience and express itself, consciousness created energy. New energy is created when a souled being becomes aware of its true nature as a creator rather than creation.

Another important transformation that is taking place parallel to your personal one is humanity's evolution. Right now the spiritual evolution of humanity is closely linked with the technological advancements taking place. Within just thirty years, technology will develop in such drastic proportions that the very pillars upon which society are built will tumble. The way in which we define ourselves as human beings, and how we perceive ourselves as humans, will change in revolutionary proportions. Whereas before this shift only took place internally within the awakening human, in the near future this questioning of 'what a human being is' will take place globally, affecting all of humanity. Especially the advancements taking place in the field of artificial intelligence will highlight the importance of consciousness. Consciousness no longer is a question concerning merely philosophers and spiritual movements; consciousness will become the core of all fundamental questions relating to technology and science. The gurus of modern science and technology speak about 'singularity', referring to a point in time in the near future when we can no longer foresee the future based on past events. It is a point when the mathematical formulas that were used to calculate future advancements no longer hold true because artificial intelligence surpasses human intelligence, and thus keeps improving itself beyond patterns of human development. Awakening might just be the best way to stay sane in an era of unprecedented technological and societal leaps.

Although physically the Earth is one planet and all of humanity is seemingly experiencing life on the same Earth, from the standpoint of consciousness there are several strata or dimensions of Earth. On each strata, reality is experienced more or less consciously, more or less dualistic. So what does this mean for those of us who choose to experience the 'New Earth' that already exists? It means, from what I have discovered so far, that the old energy is still present, including the polarity and contrast that comes with it, and at the same time another consciousness is starting to blossom on Earth. It is up to each of us, in each moment, to choose which reality to live in. We have the freedom to choose to live in a stratum of consciousness where we prioritise inner peace and presence over the distractions, seduction and craziness of the world around us. The more unpredictable the world around us becomes, the more important it is to release attachments to the external and strengthen our connection to our inner self.

New Energy is a complex topic, partly because it is so new that we don't have many words to describe it yet. It is a new element that consciousness explorers and quantum physicist are currently researching. One thing that is apparent, however, is that the division between these two or more types of consciousness (duality-based consciousness and more expanded consciousness) seems to be growing on the planet. When your life doesn't move in patterns anymore, but from one inspiration to the next, from breath to breath and feeling to feeling, you'll know that new energy has entered your life. Remember, new energy is really just wisdom in expression. Here are some observations about the new energy, based on my studies and my experiences of working with conscious manifestation:

• New energy doesn't respect patterns or predictable repetitions. You can't measure, predict or put it into a formula for the simple reason that it transcends limitations. It's an element without apparent order. This means that it will feel and manifest itself differently every single day, and expand with you. New energy today might feel different to new energy tomorrow.

• New energy exists regardless of the evolution of humanity and technology. It is not dependent on any technology.

• It's not scientific, yet it is a potential reality. It doesn't operate in the usual action-reaction equation, and you don't need to understand it to work with it.

• It is expansive and free. It isn't fuelled by force, power, duality or friction. Instead, it responds to allowing, clarity, and choices made without agenda; in other words, it responds to pure consciousness. If you want to manifest something using new energy, make sure to remove any power dynamics (such as drama, fear, ego, etc.) out of the situation, remembering that you, and everyone else involved in your creation, carries no blame.

• There is no friction between light and darkness in the new energy. This means that being attached to ideas of what is good and bad, as well as any judgments, will prevent you from experiencing new energy. In the new energy, the light and the dark are co-existing in a complementary, but neutral state.

• It cannot be manipulated into doing your will (it is not black magic), but it naturally serves you once you release any agenda for a specific outcome. This requires trusting yourself implicitly.

• It is playful and light, yet can be very potent. Familiarise yourself with it by inviting it into your dreams, into your imagination and meditation, and into your every-day life.

• It will not act or react the way you've come to expect energy to act. It doesn't follow the principle of cause and effect.

In fact, it will bring you solutions before you even detect a problem, and if you have a question it will provide an answer so new that you might miss it.

• It respects your sovereignty. In other words, as long as you resist life, it will adapt to your limitations. However, if you truly allow, it will flow without lack or restraint. Whenever you feel limitations, breathe consciously until you feel your walls of resistance melting.

• You don't need a middleman to access it and you don't need to earn it. It comes to you directly as soon as you choose to acknowledge and trust your inherent creative nature.

• New energy operates beyond time and space, yet it can affect this physical reality. When you want to create something from the new energy perspective, release any expectations about when or how the creation will manifest.

• It is already here, and it can be experienced in the now-moment by being present and anchored in your 'body of consciousness'.

• When you invite the new energy consciously into your life, you are co-creating the New Earth consciousness while being embodied here on old Earth – if you dare to be a pioneer of new energy.

The topic of new energy is very interesting and worth exploring more, however it's not the focus of this book. I've merely shared a glimpse into this new terrain, because it is something that we naturally stumble upon on our path to realization. We don't have to wait for the revolution of artificial intelligence to make a quantum leap. We only need consciousness and a choice to allow the new. No matter what happens on this Earth, and how far technology will advance, always remember that you have consciousness; no technology, no being, not even nature itself or death can take consciousness away from you, because your essence is consciousness. Consciousness – that organic intelligence of the soul – might appear uncertain, illogical and subtle compared to artificial intelligence (both the kind found in technology and the A.I. of our human brains), but consciousness has that invaluable, often overlooked element that brings grace and resolution to any situation: wisdom. Wisdom is what makes your humanity divine and your divinity unique.

Now that I've shared my perspective on this experience of awakening and enlightenment, it is your turn to write your own insights and ideas into the mosaic of your realization. The next part of the book presents interviews with other pioneers of consciousness, each modern master sharing his or her unique story of awakening. Hopefully you will understand through these various stories that you are neither alone nor crazy even though you are awakening in a world that is mostly asleep – though you might be a bit of a spiritual revolutionary.

Part 4

Modern Masters

This part of the book consists of six in-depth interviews with eight awakened humans from various parts of the world. The purpose of these interviews is to give you a glimpse into the reality of these living masters and to portray the uniqueness of each person's path into awakening. There are as many paths to realization as there are awakening humans, and hopefully these interviews serve to inspire you to trust your path with crystalline clarity. In addition, my purpose was to demonstrate that enlightenment or self-actualization doesn't belong only to spiritual gurus, but is available to anyone who is committed to their freedom – regardless of their cultural, ethnic, religious, academic, professional or ancestral background and regardless of their age and gender. None of the interviewees are well-known spiritual teachers (at the time of writing this book), although they share their wisdom with others in various ways. So now, I'd like to invite you to sit back and enjoy your reading experience!

Sandra Lamut and Danijel Trstenjak

Sandra and Danijel are two inspiring entrepreneurs
from Slovenia. At the time of the interview, both still had
conventional 9-5 jobs.

Sandra is in love with nature, life and her partner Danijel. On
the way of exploring her unlimited and unconditional Self she
met with different kinds of Eastern and Western techniques
and tools. They helped her to explore her own being and her
role here on Earth and in the universe. She is a facilitator for
The Stargate Experience and a gifted facilitator for unique
physical exercises. Sandra is a pure channel for the Divine
Feminine energy that comes through in the Stargate sessions.
She organizes different events on topics related to conscious
living with teachers from all over the world. Sandra is a
founder of the Institute of Conscious Life and co-founder of
the brand Connected (www.connected.si/). In her own life, she
is exploring conscious living through her roles as a mother,
partner, friend, teacher, disciple and Divine Being.

Danijel is a gifted artist and author, drawn to express his
experiences through different forms, provided by nature,
giving his creations both artistic and practical value. In 2015,
he decided to quit his regular job and started to do whatever
felt right in the moment. The only indicator for him was to
feel happy and fulfilled in the process. A huge boost of new
inspiration came in to create amazing hand-painted energy
symbols on stones, called 'Gaialits' - powerful healing and
energizing stones, acknowledged by people from around the
world.

He also started to build traditional wooden bows, carving them carefully into aesthetic and useful tools for practicing focus and internal alignment. Danijel's ability to feel and translate supportive energies into visual and verbal images opened new doors to work on several projects as copywriter and designer. He is also the co-founder of the brand Connected.

The Journey into Awakening

Kim: Can you share about your early experiences of awakening?

Sandra: My experience is that awakening is very exciting but challenging, and there is a purpose in that. I felt this [inner] calling for awakening when I was 14 years old when I read some books and later started going to many seminars and workshops. The journey is challenging because of the changes that one goes through with awakening. Everything I went through within was mirrored in the outside world. So, for a long time what I saw mirrored in outside circumstances didn't feel good. When you accept this journey as your priority and make that choice to reach higher frequencies and choose to live a peaceful, blessed and joyful life, you have to make some changes and find out how to put your heaven on Earth. This is our purpose, as is the quest to know who we are, to discover our soul, and to remember that we are humans but also exist on many other dimensions. This can be hard to accept, to recognize that this is actually real – we are more than "just" human. It truly is a journey. Maybe the young generations will arrive there much faster, because now the energies are different from when we were born…

Living in Trust

Kim: What does self-trust mean to you and how have you developed it?

Sandra: Every minute of the day is an opportunity to focus on the "I am –state". Situations come and I have to remind myself to trust that I know what I need in that moment. The most important thing is to be aware when I don't feel good and to consciously try to transform that state. A few years ago, these feelings of sadness and such took a much longer time to move through, nowadays I process this quickly. It's important to have somebody close-by to whom you can talk and share about your emotions, to help you see where you are stuck. The self-trust grows as I become more and more conscious of how I feel. This journey is a choice that takes place every moment of the day.

I say to myself every day: "trust yourself, be aware of your own wisdom". I believe that we have all the wisdom within us; that you can be the channel for yourself, and that you know everything you need to know. Especially when we trust ourselves 100%. Still, it's supportive to have these other beings around, and to know that you're not alone, especially during those times when we forget to trust that we *are* humans and masters.

Danijel: In this past year, there were so many indicators that it's time for me to trust *myself* above all. In the beginning, I didn't listen to them. They were small things, like an intuition to pick a different route with the car, and then my mind would question that and I would take the old, usual route that logically made more sense. Then there would be heavy traffic and I would stand still for one hour. And this happened repeatedly. Imagine the stupidity of falling into the same trap over and over again...

That's why I say: Listen to yourself; it doesn't matter where it brings you, and it doesn't matter if you make a mistake. You make mistakes anyway, even when you don't listen to your intuition – what have you got to lose? Slowly I'm starting to trust in myself more and to listen to that inner wisdom. The distractions and doubts still come up sometimes; like a train, it's hard to change direction. As humans we are so addicted to somebody else's advice or suggestions. One day I realized that my whole life was based on suggestions made by others. 45 years of my life, just suggested by other people. "Where have I been? Can I please live my own life now?" I thought. If I want to live my own life, I have to trust in myself. There is no Buddha, Allah, or Jesus who could give me better advice than I can give to myself. After all, this is my divine plan, I created and chose my life, chose what I have to learn in this life. If anybody else is trying to bring me through my life, they are doing it from their subjective truth. It's all about approaching the same source of wisdom that is available and same for everyone. If we allow ourselves to open up to this source directly, not through a channel or someone else, the energy remains purer. Then the knowledge that you receive is more individualized to your own needs.

Dealing with Doubt

Kim: How do you deal with doubt?

Sandra: It can be hard to deal with doubt. It helps to have Danijel and friends with whom I can talk, to allow support from others. Otherwise I can just go around in my head and remain stuck in one perspective. When I share, I see more easily where I'm stuck. I don't want to stay in those feelings of doubt, but they will come, after all we live on Earth. Doubt is inevitable, but the important thing is that you can learn to move through it fast. The key is awareness (of the doubt), because then you can start working on it. With practise, you become faster at transforming the doubt. In time, I believe, these self-doubts will almost disappear. I can see myself going into that direction.

Managing the Split of Work and Spirituality

Kim: Having a conventional job while unravelling every part within you that is stuck in patterns – how do you deal with it?

Sandra: Lately it has been harder for me to go to my job (edit: accounting), which is really a very mental job, because I can see how it affects the amplitude of my frequency: For example, I feel very inspired in the morning after having done some physical exercise or a short meditation. But then I start my workday, engage in all this mental activity, and I can feel how the frequency is dropping. I have to consciously focus on being present, so that my frequency doesn't fall too low. So, it takes a conscious focus while being at work. On most days of the week I feel the need to meditate to keep the vibrations high. Raising my frequency is a priority for me, however, it's tiring to be in this state of up and down, so I'm really planning to change my job because of that.

Awakened Relationships

Kim: Could you share about your experiences of being in a relationship while going through the awakening journey?

Sandra: Partnership is not for granted. You have to know yourself and learn to know the other person *as they are*. In many ways, Danijel and I are totally different from each other, and in some ways very similar. So we have to find the balance between us. We are together in the partnership as two *individuals*. We allow each other to be themselves. This can be hard, because it's natural to start thinking or feeling like the partner does, but in the end, he's not me and I'm not him. Communication is very important: continually checking in on how your partner feels.

Danijel: Healthy partnership grows out of self-trust. If you don't trust yourself, then you depend on your partner for suggestions, opinions, and self-worth. In such a dynamic, one always has to be the stronger one, the leader, and the other person is the follower. This leads to a competition, a power-play of the ego, and then you lose the real purpose of being together. For me the purpose of a partnership is all about mirroring. The partner is holding you a mirror. Because when you are alone, you see your own issues less clearly. The partner shows you the parts of yourself that are not yet integrated. The areas of yourself where you still hold "lower vibrations". This is okay if you are capable of accepting it. If you're not aware of this or ready to accept it, the fights begin. "You're like this and not that, why can't you be more that", you start blaming each other... When the partnership goes into this phase, it's better just to separate for a while and get back in tune with yourself. Otherwise it will turn into an ego-fight, and that will never be resolved, because the ego feeds on these fights.

Sandra: Partners have to be supportive to each other.

Danijel: I have to admit: in the beginning, when we came together, I was trying to shape Sandra into something that I thought would be appropriate – old patterns that I had inherited from my parents – but then Sandra didn't want to do it. It was a surprise: she just wanted to be herself and said to me, "you should consider who you want to be, also"! The question is: Why do you need the people around you to do things the way you think they should be done?

You engage in the act of seeking approval from others when you don't trust yourself and instead trust the approval of the people around you: if they approve, everything's fine; if they don't, you question what you did wrong… But where am I in this story? If I didn't trust myself, I'd need Sandra to always approve of me. And if she doesn't approve, if she doesn't give me energy (and my ego is hungry for this energy), this could make me mentally violent and I would try to force her to approve my actions. It's just about feeding energies from other people. When we trust ourselves, we don't have to try to change others – live and let others live the way they want to live. Then you don't depend on others anymore. This is what we learnt in our relationship over 15 years.

Sandra: In the beginning it was hard, but somehow we knew that we were meant to be together and that somehow we'll figure out why we are together. The main thing is that we are growing together as individuals and also as a partnership.

Danijel: Because we are so different from each other, accepting each other and our differences means that we are evolving as individuals. We realized that on our own, with very little help from the outside. This partnership is something that I'm very proud of because it could have gone into pieces a thousand times, but it didn't. We managed to be mature enough and conscious enough to come through these issues.

Sandra: It was not just about making our partnership survive. We are really becoming more conscious through this partnership.

Inviting New Dynamics into a Relationship

Sandra: I think it's a live process; every minute the relationship is alive. It can be truly challenging, but I also believe that in a relationship we evolve much faster than as individuals.

Danijel: …Because we have a mirror. This is the purpose of a partnership, that you can accept the mirror, through the loving acceptance of your partner.

Sandra: There are hard moments. But it's important how you get through these moments. To talk about the process, why did these emotions rise up and so on… It's important to get over your ego and try to understand the other person, what he or she is feeling and trying to communicate to you.

Danijel: At the same time, we also challenge each other's nerves. It's an on-going process. A relationship is not like falling into a soft meditation, it's a constant adjustment that makes you flexible and open, and in time makes you a "better" person.

Sandra: It's important when your partner doesn't feel good, for example, that you let him express this and that we together try to find a solution or another perspective. It's really important to support each other. You have to allow the emotions to rise up, only then can they be transformed, and you have to do it alone. But the partner can show you another potential.

Danijel: in the end, it's still your own choice how you feel. Sometimes it's best to let the other person be by himself/herself until they have moved through the emotion, and talk about it later from a more balanced space.

Finding your Own Tune

Kim: *What has been the most challenging thing about your awakening experience?*

Danijel: For me the most challenging part was that I didn't know what to do to be happy. My whole life was based on suggestions made by other people, and I didn't really feel into my own way, into what my mission in life is. Really the most difficult part has been (and still is) feeling a lack of purpose, not feeling useful, the lack of creativity. If there is lack of purpose in life, then you are so lost. Then this life can become such a labyrinth of darkness.

However, now it is a bit easier because I feel some direction about where I want to go. Slowly my chosen purpose is revealing itself. And this is such a relief compared to the times when I was completely blind to it. Everything was so foggy... And now I feel new possibilities approaching, for me to do something that I like to do. A lot of fear is disappearing and I'm almost ready to make a step into the unknown. Leaving your old job and knowing where you will start to work tomorrow is not really a step into the unknown. It's a change but it's not the unknown. For me it's not like this; I don't know where my next income is going to come from, but my inner situation now is that I'm willing and ready to take this step. I just have to show the courage to take this step.

Finding the Courage for Change

Kim: What has helped you find courage amidst the challenges of awakening?

Danijel: Every situation in my life was designed for me to first go deeper into the dissatisfaction, into what I don't want, until I almost hit the ground and came to the point that you I couldn't continue living in the same way any longer. That's when you are able to make the changes and throw away a lot of the limitations that were holding you in the unhappiness. Once you let go of the limitations, new things can come into your life; new energy starts to create changes on a very deep level. Like a snowball, the changes start small and become bigger and bigger. It's step-by-step process; you just wake up one day and the world looks a little bit different, and this keeps happening. You have to be open to the small changes, and then the big ones come naturally. Until you are ready for the small changes, everything stays essentially the same.

Time Traveling

Kim: If you went back in time to meet your younger self at the darkest times of your awakening, what would you say to them?

Sandra: In the past and still today, whenever I face my hidden darkest feelings, I consciously talk with myself, with my inner child: "My dear »Sandrica« (that's how I call my inner child), I know you are afraid (sad, angry, alone, judgmental ...) at this moment, but nothing seems as it appears. Just let it all go! I am here for you, you are not alone! Everything is OK. I love you and honour you! You are not just this body, you are a vast being connected to All that Is, to the source of Love!" It calms me and makes me feel good and it also helps me to see the so called "problem" or emotion from a different perspective. For me it is also the fastest way to get out of this state, of this lower frequency. My main life focus is to raise my vibration, my consciousness. I am grateful when my dark side comes out from the subconscious, so that I can let it go or transform it and trust where the next step is going to lead me.

Danijel: I would say, "Celebrate those moments of feeling bad, because you allowed some stuck energy to come to the surface for you to see it and release it from your system. Just let it go – for it is already leaving and not important any more. What is important is to just keep on moving, following your highest excitement and enjoying the ride.

Romana Ercegović, Ph.D.

Romana, from Slovenia, is an explorer and creator of new ways of conscious, soulful theatre art – a playwright, theatre director, actress, facilitator of transformative creative retreats, storyteller, poet, author of children's literature, puppet performances and mother of a 12-year old boy. She creates original solo performances in her *Sacred Theater* and is also the director of *The Royal Shaumbra Theater,* an international group of passionate researchers of new energy creativity.

Romana chose an independent artistic path and follows her vision of theatre, which awakens the perception of beauty, magic and joy of life, and honours the balance between the feminine and the masculine, and celebrates the connection to Nature. She has devoted the last 17 years to researching the ancient understandings of art, sacred ceremonies and ancient mysteries (mystery schools) of different cultures – with the intention of developing a new approach to theatre, where theatre art can again be used as a tool for the inner experience of divinity and the sacredness of Life.

To discover more about Romana, please visit her website: romanaercegovic.com

Intuition and New Energy Research

Kim: What does it mean for you to be connected to your intuition?

Romana: For me intuition is a kind of flow of wisdom, of the knowingness that is always present on some level of my awareness. What is important for me in my life is to be connected to this flow as much as I can be. I see this flow as a divine knowingness that is tailored particularly for my purpose, and related to whatever is important for me to know in this specific moment. And I really use it through all kinds of activities, for creative or daily activities, even for research. For example, when I was writing my thesis, I allowed my intuition to lead me to the sources in literature or in books that confirmed the information I had received through visions. In such a way, I connected the intuitive information (which is the most reliable source of information for me) with the earthly plane. Also, my performances, such as *Mary Magdalene, White Buffalo Woman, Persephone* and others, are always based first on intuition and vision, and supported by research from other sources.

Visions and Sacred Timing

Kim: How do you reach this space where you are receptive to visions?

Romana: I practiced a lot in the past 15 or more years. In the beginning, I would need particular conditions to receive visions, such as travelling, being in a place that is connected to my past lives or to history. The visions are often related to past lives or ideas for my future creations. Usually these visions come when I am alone, or with people in whose company I feel very safe. Sometimes, I would prepare myself by doing a ceremony inspired by the Native American 'vision quest': By going into solitude, into the nature for a few days, sometimes even fasting. Removing all the distractions. Later this wasn't necessary, since the veils were getting much thinner.

I have always approached things in my own way, in a more

gentle, feminine, allowing way rather than through suffering and discipline. Conscious breathing can also help. Usually I don't receive visions when I'm very active in the outer world or in social life; they require taking time to be with myself. These visions always come at the right time, and they don't necessarily come when I want them to come. Or sometimes the visions are about a different topic than I expect or wish for. It's about sacred timing: My soul is in charge and knows when I'm ready to get a particular insight about something. It's not about satisfying my curiosity. It's also helpful to allow the imagination to come in, allowing myself to imagine what I would really love to do, what could really fulfil me. Asking (with an open heart), "what do I really wish for?" is a wonderful way of opening to vision. "What would I choose if I could have anything I wanted?" Visions are about allowing ourselves to create purely out of joy, just for ourselves.

Kim: You seem to have a very playful approach to intuition.

Romana: My background is rather serious, I was very connected with the Native American culture and felt a lot of responsibility for the Earth, and for humanity. There was much seriousness in my early years of awakening, and gradually I have been releasing this. When I'm connected to the more subtle realities or dimensions, there is always a lot of joy. In 2003, I used my vision to visit the circle of Ascended Masters for the first time, and met Yeshua, Djwal Khul and others. I was surprised that, although they were concerned about the Earth and humanity, they weren't worried or serious about it; they were just radiating pure joy and love. They were full of humour and laughter. Now this is obvious to me, but back then this was a big surprise and a relief.

Silence and Solitude

Kim: How do you use the tools of silence and solitude?

Romana: That's something very precious to me, even being in the presence of others in silence, and share presence in that way: Just looking someone in the eyes, without talking, just feeling their depth, being together and, at the same time, being present with yourself. This is the art of true communication. Even by spending just one hour of silence, you can get to another level of being connected with yourself.

My need for isolation is based on my character; I get very easily attuned with the energies of the people around me and I intuitively adapt to the energies of the people around me. Sometimes I lose clarity of what *I* feel in that moment, because I'm very sensitive so I easily pick up the energies of others. Being alone enables me to really be in my own energy. I know that for some people this isn't a problem, they can be in their own energies no matter who is around. That's not the case with me; I can come close to someone and then have to take some distance again. I have to consciously dance this dance, otherwise I get lost in other people's energies. Silence is not only a way to connect with my intuition, but also a way to rejuvenate and centre myself.

The Gifts of Journaling

Kim: How has the practice of journaling supported you in this journey of awakening?

Romana: Journaling is a great tool for grounding experiences.

Particularly after I've had a strong experience, or a clear message from my soul, then I write it down so that it becomes more grounded, more solid in my reality. Of course, it also helps me to remember. When I'm in a state where I don't feel connected to my intuition, just reading previous entries draws me back into my own awareness. It reminds me to come back to myself again. I also use journaling for my creative projects: Usually these projects come together like a puzzle, and I collect parts of the puzzle pieces from different sources and experiences. Journaling is helpful in showing me a structure, the big picture, bringing different pieces of the puzzle together. Journaling can help make sense of intuitive messages.

The New Art of Parenting

Kim: What is important for you as a conscious parent?

Romana: What I consider most important (as a parent) is to really nourish this bond between the child and the parent – I'm a single mother. To really feel into this being… I don't really look at him as a child, but as a wise soul, who sometimes needs a bit of directing. For me the art of parenting is to stay in tune with this soul within him, and at the same time be conscious of all the aspects of this soul that might be less conscious. I have to be discerning about when it's time to support his sovereignty, and when it's appropriate to limit him, for example when his aspects would demand something, or try to put me down, try to manipulate. The art of parenting, as is the art of communication with others, is really about being conscious and awake regarding what is happening in the now moment. Of course, I nourish the loving bond between him and me, I tell and show him often that I love and respect him, but I don't want to create any dependence, conditioning or other energy feeding dynamics – as far as I'm aware of them. We have a lot of fun together, a lot of conversations, sometimes also disagreements. I'm not really fond of these ideas that you have to be there *all the time* for your child; I really appreciate my time alone.

Trusting the Path

Kim: What has been most challenging for you regarding your awakening?

Romana: For me maybe the hardest part of awakening was the beginning of my awakening journey, because I was feeling so alone. In 1996, when all these internal changes started happening to me and I felt a need to remove myself from the outer world, I felt so overwhelmed with my relationships and with my own heaviness. It was overwhelming to see things that others didn't, and when I spoke about them, others simply didn't get it. Seeing outside of the box, and others looking at me strangely. It was during the time when I was finishing my bachelor degree at the Theatre Academy of Ljubljana. At that time, I was awakening to concepts such as higher needs for the world and what is the meaning of what we are doing, what this life is all about, why I'm here, what's the meaning of the art… At the time, I didn't realize that maybe other people were limited in their perspective, I just felt that I was too heavy, too much, too expanded.

I needed to retreat, and that's what I did. I moved to live with myself, separated from my long-term boyfriend, and realized how trapped I had been in that relationship. Of course, emotionally it was really hard to let that relationship go, but on the other hand I just knew that I needed to be free to expand. Otherwise I would explode within myself. So I just cut myself away from many friends, and from the theatre career. I needed a lot of time by myself. I was so much in need for my own safe space, so overwhelmed simply by being around other people that, for a while, I decided to sleep during the day and be awake at night. I turned off my telephone, and started to live like a monk.

During that time, I was writing my diploma and spending my time mostly with books, and sometimes walking in parks. My thesis was about 'the new templates for the perfection of art'. What are the real templates for art? I was writing about the vibrational perfection of art; about how the vibration of love emanating from an artwork is the real criterion of perfection of an artwork. Of course, my professors didn't approve of my thesis, in fact one of them regarded my thesis as the most confused diploma that he ever saw. And for me it felt like I'm being burned at the stake again, being accused of thinking differently. I didn't compromise the core of my thesis, but I made it more systematic and changed the form of how it was written. And eventually, because I was a very good student and had good grades in most subjects, the committee couldn't totally ignore it and ended up giving me the lowest possible grade with which I passed.

I felt so much love in my heart for this work, and I really trusted it. On the other hand, I felt like a total alien in this world. I felt very ridiculed by other artists, ex-friends... For example, my best friend back then told me that she didn't believe in me. But I just saw this light in front of me. I also felt Native American spirits supporting me, who revealed themselves to me in the very beginning of my awakening process, when I felt overwhelmed. One day in the bath, I saw a face of a Native American elder woman, and she said to me: "Don't worry, we are following your steps, you are not alone." That's all she said. I didn't know who she was. Later I realized that they are spiritual elders, my guides, who were with me for the next several years, until it was time for me to go forward alone. I was so naïve back then, almost 20 years ago, so innocent in a way, but in this naivety I was very bold. I felt an inner strength, as if nobody could do anything to me.

Later on, in the following years, aspects of guilt, doubt, self-accusation and self-criticism came out, and also abundance and self-worth issues, just name it... Other challenging events followed, like my first husband choosing to kill himself, and ten years later the separation between my second husband and me. Although these events that happened later were difficult, I understood things more by then. I understood that death doesn't exist, it's just a transformation of energy. I was also beginning to understand that there are many layers of reality and I didn't identify only with my human self any more...

This awakening process was difficult, yet somehow, because I was aware of the presence of my divine self, I always considered myself very strong. I just knew that I could survive whatever comes, that I had chosen such a bloody different part to play compared to so many other people. I knew I had to follow and trust my inner feeling, my intuition, no matter what... Everything becomes easier after that.

Redefining what it Means to be a Woman

Romana: One of my greatest challenges was, and in a way still is, being in a relationship and, at the same time, have the connection with my inner core, my wisdom, my own rhythm. I believe this is one of my ways of experiencing freedom: finding this balance of who I am as a sovereign being, and who I am in relationship to others, particularly in intimate relationships; liberating all these conventional ideas about relationships and the role of the woman, how I should be as a woman. As I am walking this path of being connected to the "divine feminine", I am also walking through my own experiences, and facing all the old belief systems of what it means to be a woman. On some level, I chose to go through all these dysfunctional patterns in order to, finally some day, come to this point of experiencing and expressing a healthy feminine energy and a healthy balance of feminine and masculine energies both within and without.

Conscious Art

Kim: In your perspective, what is the meaning of art?

Romana: We can walk a path of beauty if we choose to...

What this means to me, as an artist, is the importance of revealing and expressing the beauty of nature and of humans, to show the depth of this beauty. Expressing beauty might seem like activity without political, economic or moral sense. What are we doing as artists? Revealing the beauty. But we are doing this because we believe that bringing these potentials of beauty, balance, and harmony reveals a different perspective on life, and that *is* socially engaging.

Time Traveling

Kim: What is the most important message you would give your younger Self?

Romana: For me, one of the most important messages would be to accept myself as I am, and to accept the world as it is, in all its imperfections. I have always felt or known a greater potential for how things *could be*, who I am at core, how the world could be. And then being born into *this* dense, chaotic, imbalanced reality with so much rubbish and stupidity, and to see all these aspects within me as well, is hard. To finally accept others and myself as we are, and realizing that I don't need to change anything, is a relief.

To remember that I just have this beautiful, amazing opportunity to make my life as enjoyable as possible, and what actually makes it enjoyable for me, is to be in this state of grace and love myself as much as I can. Being aware enough to choose that state more and more often, more consciously. Being aware that this life can be a playground of so much beauty. Being aware that I can manifest this beauty no matter of the harshness of the world as it is; I can create my own world according to how I would like to experience it. The bigger wisdom is that my vision of how I would like to experience life and the world, doesn't depend on anyone else! I enjoy sharing this playfulness and sharing the creation with others, but I'm not dependent on sharing it...Of course, part of the joy of life is to dance together, to co-create and to really live in this world with the awareness that I've made myself happy and along with that inspired other people as well.

When I was younger, I felt so much responsibility for this world, for other people. Even as a child I could feel other people's pain and I was taking those emotions into me. I felt so much love and compassion, but didn't know how to deal with that. So I would tell my inner girl that she can run around joyfully, allow herself to fly on wings of imagination instead of taking on the burdens of others. I would tell her how to keep a safe and sacred space within and how to share her love consciously.

On the other hand, I know that even if I knew all that back then, I would still need time to truly distil and embody this wisdom. Now I understand that life is simple, but this realization comes after understanding the complexity within, the passionate dance of darkness and light. It takes a lot of time; at least for me, it took a lot of experiences to become a simple master. There has always been so much passion and compassion within me, and when I was younger, I didn't always know how to combine those two qualities and deal with them. Either I got burned by my fire or I supressed it. I felt my complexity as a burden. Now I know it's a blessing. I'm not saying that I'm always gracefully embodying all that wisdom in my everyday life, but I know more and more clearly how to handle myself – how to be a director to the various actors/aspects in my rich inner theatre on the stage of Life. And I'm even to able to laugh out loud, to have great fun on the stage, symbolically and also literally in theatre, which has remained one of the greatest loves of my life.

Jascha Beck

Jascha is consciously living in his own creation of life. In his human life, he worked many years as a TV journalist. Today Jascha loves to inspire people in their awakening and in becoming aware of their mastery. As a German-born he is especially used to the difficulties of a dense mind with all its fears and struggles. Going beyond the mind and expressing the freedom of the true self is the essence of this lifetime.

Early Awakening Experiences

Kim: Jascha, how did the journey of awakening begin for you?

Jascha: From the point where I am standing now, I can see that my whole life was about awakening and realization. Of course, in my childhood and youth I didn't recognize what I was experiencing as awakening. I didn't have the awareness to see that, but now I do. I had always this inner drive, this deep, deep wish and longing for freedom. It began as a child: I recognized that something was wrong, I loved my family and they loved me, but I could feel that what I saw and experienced wasn't the end, wasn't my truth. My life was just an act where I was in. I couldn't understand what it was all about; I could just see that it was not right in a way, because I was looking for *freedom*. It was as if I had, coming into this lifetime, set my inner navigation system on freedom as my destiny or destination. My inner guidance led me there, despite me not understanding what was happening.

When I was in my late twenties, early thirties, much awareness started coming to me about who I am. There was a situation in my family, an addiction, and I was very connected with this person (my mother) and I was very much suffering with her. We were so closely connected; my mother had taught me that love is possessive (of course not in a conscious way, but it was the way that she had been taught and so she passed it onto me). When she was feeling bad, I had to feel bad, too. That led to a situation that was unbearable for me. She was in so much pain, and with other situations that were happening at the time, it was like the light went out in my life. Something had to change.

Before the situation was very unbearable, I had one out-of-body experience, like a prelude to the true awakening that happened afterwards. I had just moved from Munich to Berlin for a new job and I didn't have my own apartment yet, so I was living at a friend's house. This friend said to me: "Of course you can stay here, but you should know that there are ghosts in this house." I didn't really believe him. But that night I was lying in my bed, between awake and asleep, and suddenly I felt a hand grabbing me at my throat. I was so frightened that I was literally thrown out of my body. It felt like I was being shaken around, and the next moment everything was quiet and peaceful. I was still conscious of myself but there was no fear, no emotions, and the room looked a bit different yet it was the same room, and then I could see my body lying there. That felt very strange; not fearful, but curious. And then I just felt the inclination to go back into my body. Slowly I placed my awareness back in my body, and again I felt a shaking and then I was back. This was a very deep experience for me, because it made me ask a lot of questions: what had happened, who am I, and so on.

Soon another strong turning point in my life occurred: I was living in Berlin and it was Christmas. I had decided to drive home for Christmas, but only if my family was in harmony. I didn't want to suffer again and repeat the drama of depression and drinking. I called my mother and asked: "Are you ok, are you feeling good? Otherwise I would prefer to stay in Berlin." She said: "No no, it's ok, I'm very happy that you're coming, how great". So I went to my car, drove about 5 hours from Berlin to Nuremberg, was really looking forward to it. I arrived at my mother's house, said, "hello, here I am". I couldn't hear any answer, but I could feel something dark. I went to her bedroom, and saw her lying there as if she was dead, with bottles of alcohol lying around. I tried to talk to her, but she could almost not speak in her state. I was so angry that I decided to go back to the car and drive those five and a half hours to Berlin again. I felt so depressed, deep in sadness, and even the weather was rainy and cold. Everything was grey on the highway, until one little spot opened in the clouds with one ray of sunshine. And for me it was like a small ray of hope.

After the long drive, I immediately went to my computer to look for help for my mother. My brother and father are both psychiatrists, actually experts in helping people with depression and addiction, but they were absolutely helpless in this situation. I was searching online, but the only answer I found was that you can only help yourself. That led me to different discussion forums on the Internet. And suddenly I felt attracted to some spiritual forums, and somehow it became less about my mother and more about the spiritual things. I could feel this wave of remembering returning to me, a feeling of remembering who I am. Not everything, but I could feel a bigger part of me that had been lost before, and I felt a big relief. From this point, everything changed in my life: All the goals that I had before, my lifestyle (going to a lot of parties, having drinks, playing in the 3-D world)… From this moment on, everything changed immediately, and that was just the beginning.

Redefining Enlightenment

Kim: What does enlightenment mean for you?

Jascha: For me, enlightenment is something very simple, just the consciousness of 'I exist'; to realize that the deepest truth of 'who I am' is the awareness that 'I exist, I am that I am'. And of course, this is an awareness that goes beyond the words. In a way, it is far too simple for the human mind. After that moment of awakening, I went through all the human journeys of my lifetimes in a very short time. I was attracted to Christianity, to Buddhism, to Shamanism, to the esoteric, to all kinds of different expressions of this very simple truth. And it was like I revisited my whole journey. I connected to my experiences again, brought them home.

Enlightenment is very simple, but the beauty of it is the *expression*, and the expression has so many flavours. All the religions, and even atheism, are different flavours of expression… But at the core, it's very simple.

For me the awareness of 'I exist' is not a thought. It's just a feeling, an awareness that I exist even beyond the human form. At the core of it there is no expression, there is no energy in it. It's a silent awareness, without movement. It's a consciousness beyond the mind, beyond analysing, beyond structure. It is a knowingness that goes beyond the five human senses.

Moving Beyond Thought

Kim: What has helped you with moving beyond the thinking self into the awareness-self?

Jascha: There are many different things that have expanded my awareness. I was very connected with Indian spirituality and *satsang*, especially with Ramana Maharshi who lived in the beginning of the 20th century. He was very revolutionary in his time, because the norm in Indian spirituality was that everything is about the Guru, and Ramana Maharshi was one of the first to say that the answers are inside of you; it's about consciousness. He also said: "start with the question 'who am I?'" With this question you automatically awaken your consciousness. That question helped me, because the answer is …silence. You move beyond thoughts into trust. Of course the human has all these definitions: "I'm a man, this is my job title, bla, bla, bla". But when you go into the feeling level and ask that question, something starts to open up within you. That was one of the ways.

Another thing that helped me a lot was conscious breathing. Thoughts and the mind are the greatest distractions; they are constantly demanding attention. We are so programmed to identify with our thoughts. When I go into the conscious breath, that means to really feel the breath, how it feels sensually, in the whole body, in the belly, and feeling this flow. Suddenly I'm out of the mind, and instead in the feeling, in the awareness of my breath.

Eckhart Tolle has also helped to guide me: He said that you can observe your thoughts. This is a tremendous shift, when you shift from identifying with the thought, i.e. "this thought is me", and instead observe the thought. It's not about stopping the thoughts. At first it wasn't possible, but with time I realized that yes, I can be the observer.

Life After Awakening...

Kim: What does your day-to-day life look and feel like now?

Jascha: If someone was to observe me, I don't think they would see a big difference on the outside. The difference is in my perspective. When I wake up in the morning, I start my day with the realization that 'I exist'. One of the biggest traps when you wake up is that immediately the mind starts to be noisy, wants to take over, wants to control and guide you into the dramas, the problems and tasks of the day. So I start with the realization that I exist. For me this is the best way to start the day, because then the whole day starts evolving in a different way. That doesn't mean that I'm in this state of presence 24/7, although a part of me always is.

From my perspective, my life is a big joke right now. I love to act, to play and to have fun. The fun is that when I'm in the awareness of 'I exist', and I realize that all the other identifications that I used to have (Jascha – the party-man, who likes to drink, use drugs and have a lot of girls, or Jascha – the spiritual man, or Jascha – the professional) are just roles, they are not who I am. The difference is that in the past I was trapped in these identifications. Now I'm playing with these roles and can have fun with them. Now I have a lot of joy in my life, a lot of humour. I laugh often at myself, and see how ridiculous this life is. Not in a judgemental way, but I think that life is just about joy and jokes and acting these roles. I don't manage to be in this state all the time, but most of the time I can see my life from this perspective, and this takes so much of the heaviness and the drama away.

And as I radiate this, my experiences feel very different. These days, when I meet people from my past, I can play this role again of Jascha the party-man, for instance, and enjoy it because I no longer take it seriously. Before there was so much judgement... Now there is joy and self-love. I was so much begging for love in the past, for attention, for other people's love, and that was a really hard way to get to the point, which was to accept myself, to accept all the acts of my human self. At that time, I could not see my identities and my experiences as an act, I could not laugh at them or see them as choices. Now I can see what a great player I was.

With releasing the judgement, the guilt and the fear comes the self-love, and with that comes a lot of love for other people. And that love is returning to me. That does not mean that I'm in a la-la world all the time. It means that I also have times of anger, times of fear, times of frustration, but this is the secret: I don't get caught in these heavy emotions like I did before; I can allow the anger too, because it's absolutely important to appreciate and allow this part of life as well, to allow myself to feel it. But now there is no spiralling into depression anymore when these emotions come. I can drop into these emotions for a day or two, but I know all the time that this is just an experience and it will change again.

Time Traveling

Kim: If you had to give your younger self any advice, in the most difficult times of awakening, what would you say to yourself?

Jascha: I would say: "All is well. Just let go. Don't think so much, don't struggle so much. The problems are not real. Everything is fine, you're in the perfect situation, at the perfect time." It was said to me and I heard it, but it didn't really reach me.

Jean Tinder

Jean comes from a deep Christian background, having been born and raised in the family of a Seventh Day Adventist minister. For as long as she can remember, she has always been in close contact with Spirit and has had many experiences of deep communion over the years.

In 1997 she began channelling God, first for herself and then to share with others. As she moved forward along her spiritual journey she came to recognize that "God" came in different flavours, expressing different facets and aspects of the divine energy. Over the years Jean has worked with many angelic beings including Tobias, St. Germain, Raphael, Kuthumi, and others.

Jean's greatest passion is embodiment of the I Am, which has become the answer to her lifelong search for truth. It is a difficult and sometimes lonely journey, and she finds great joy in sharing her experiences with those on a similar path.

Obstacles on the Journey

Kim: What were your greatest obstacles throughout your awakening journey?

Jean: I think back over the many parts of my journey, and trusting myself was something very big; to make the leap of faith, to make the big changes. Something in me knew that changes had to happen, but to just make the leap and trust that I was doing the right thing, and let that be enough. Many times there was no one around me (at the time) saying, "Yes, it's okay, go ahead. You're doing the right thing, it's not a mistake". That was one of the hardest things for me. I've come to a place where I do trust myself implicitly, but that was definitely a big challenge.

Kim: I can relate to that. How did you begin to trust yourself?

Jean: My awakening process started when I was in my early 20s: I started feeling intuitively that the belief system I had grown up in didn't have anywhere near the whole picture. So I started reading a lot of books, learning about past lives and out-of-body experiences. I was raised in a belief system of "you are your body and that's all there is to you, and when you die, your body is dead, and Jesus brings you to heaven if you were good. There is nothing beyond what you can see". As I read more about people's experience in the non-physical realms, the revelation and confirmation of what I was intuitively feeling was amazing.

I had married at 18 and had two little kids. My husband was someone of very different consciousness, a good person, but quite uninterested in anything like the evolution of self. A few years into the marriage I was feeling stifled, but a good girl doesn't break up a family. So I felt for 5-6 years that I couldn't continue in this marriage, but I didn't know what to do. After ten years it finally ended, because that first process of trusting myself and going against the flow – doing everything I'm not supposed to do – took a long time. And then over the years, I began to recognize that feeling of 'I have to go in this direction or make that change'. No matter how or when this feeling would come up, I learned to trust it. I've made some pretty crazy leaps of faith based on that, but after you do it a couple of times, you realize: Well, that was quite an experience, but here I am, I'm okay, and it turned out however it turned out. You learn that the world doesn't fall apart when you trust yourself.

Taking a Leap of Faith

Kim: What did it look like for you to take those leaps of faith?

Jean: One of the biggest leaps of faith happened during my second marriage. A couple of years after splitting up I met my second husband. We immediately had a child, we joined a church, and I learned to translate the church teachings into what I felt resonated with me, which was less dogma and much closer to what Jesus taught. Then about seven years into that marriage everything started changing. I got pregnant with my daughter, and the day we got back from hospital after giving birth, the landlord showed up to inform us we had six weeks to vacate the house. I knew things were changing and shifting within me and my understandings, and that this was part of it. I like to say that life chews us up and spits us out, and so we ended up moving to a different state when my daughter was 6 weeks old, the destination determined only by the fact that we felt drawn to this town.

My husband and I were both self-employed, so the relocation wasn't too difficult. All together there were 6 of us in a little 2-bedroom apartment, and we survived there for a year and a half. By then, I knew that my husband and I had completed our very karmic agreement to reconnect. I've always said that if anyone was my soulmate, it was him, because we had so much drawing us together. It was amazing how we connected, but at some point it was complete, which was a relief to both of us, because the relationship was also challenging. He was getting interested in other people and I was feeling that it was time for me to move away. I assumed I would move to Santa Fe, where my brother lived, so I left with my 18-month-old daughter, and went on a road trip. On the way to Santa Fe, I attended a Crimson Circle event in Denver. It was magical, and while there the knowing just washed over me that *this* is home, not Santa Fe.

I went back home to pack up my life. Six weeks later my little girl and I, and my brother helping us, moved to Colorado. I found myself in a little hotel with 200 dollars to my name; with no friends, no house and no job, nothing to help me get going. And somehow I'm still here. I had nothing waiting for me in Colorado, no support system, yet through a series of small miracles and total trust, I made it. I'm still here, and I'm doing fine. When that internal passion and knowing pulls me in a certain direction, I know to listen to it. And I know it always works out.

Life as Embodied Consciousness

Kim: How does it feel now that you've started to embody your consciousness? What do you do every day to anchor this consciousness? What does your life look like now?

Jean: My life now looks very much like I envisioned it many years ago. When I first moved to Colorado, I managed to move into a small house and had lots of Shaumbra[16] come to visit

---

16   "The name used by Tobias and others for the group of humans going

me. I was starving for that connection and would spend a lot of time at my computer doing online chatting because, at the time, it was all about connecting and realizing that there are other people like me, all over the world! During all this time at my computer writing in the chatrooms, I thought: Ah, if only I could make a living working at my computer, because I loved it! And that's exactly what I do now: I work at home, spend up to 10 hours a day at the computer, and make my living from it.

Throughout my journey, I also allowed myself to acknowledge that I'm a channeller. It was very scary at first. I had been talking to Spirit privately for many years in my journal, and at some point, it turned into what I do now, which is channelling for people verbally. That took some practice. Regarding a daily practice, in the past I've spent time breathing or meditating, doing different things, and over the years I have embodied it all. In other words, now I *feel* when I'm getting all caught up in my head, when I'm getting stressed or confused, and I just know to take a few deep breaths, come back to myself, come back to my feelings, and most importantly, to trust. If I'm working too hard at something, if my energies are all tangled up in a task, for example, or something that I'm working on isn't flowing, I just let it go, disengage, and it finds resolution by itself. Whether it's a stubborn aspect that I'm trying to integrate, or a project that I'm trying to do, I would say that my daily life is just a flow of feeling: Feeling what's the next project or next thing to do. I don't follow a tight schedule (obviously I do have some responsibilities that are scheduled), and I don't follow any kind of routine or practice other than just myself in

through the awakening process." Source: www.crimsoncircle.com/More/Glossary

the moment, doing what I want to do. I love my work, and that is most of what I do. It inspires me nearly every day.

Beyond Goal Setting – How to Create in the New Energy

Kim: I am now exploring letting go of goals, which is huge because we are so conditioned to be always moving toward some achievements and goals. So you just follow your feeling in the moment without setting goals?

Jean: It's funny that you mention goals, because how I live now is pretty much exactly how I dreamed of living, but it didn't come by setting it as a goal. Back in 2007, I took the Dreamwalker Ascension Class with Adamus Saint-Germain, and became a teacher for that. During the class, there is a point where you answer a question about 4 things that you want to create. When I did the workshop, the first thing on my list was that I want a home in the mountains. At the time, I was still self-employed, I had launched my Creator Cards and, of course, my channelling sessions, but I was still living barely getting by: barely enough money, sometimes not enough; barely paying rent. So when I made that choice I thought, "Oh my gosh, how am I ever going to create a home in the mountains? But that is what I want, what I choose", so I just let it be. Then over the next couple of years, I found that I can't work towards something if it goes against what I want to do, or what I feel in the moment; for me it doesn't work anymore to force myself into something or to work towards a goal. Besides, I didn't even know how to work towards getting a house in the mountains. It was impossible, as far as practical things go. A few months later, I was offered the job that I have now with the Crimson Circle, and I moved to Nevada and lived there for a year and worked at the office. Then it was time for the CC to close the office and move back to Colorado, and I very magically and synchronistically found a home in the mountains, which is now where I live. Looking back, there is nothing I could have done, no goal I could have set to make it happen. I didn't say: I want a home in the mountains, and I will do this and this and this to make it happen. Everything was so magical and synchronistic, appearing in my life by trusting myself in the moment, even though I went in some unexpected directions before I got here.

That's how you get to where you want: by always following the desire of your heart and the inspiration of the moment. Your soul knows what you want, your soul knows what's coming; you don't have to figure it out. You just have to follow that inner compass, and it always gets you to the most amazing places. Instead of goals, I have the choice in each moment to follow what I feel, what inspires me, and it leads me on quite a magical path. I couldn't have planned it or set goals to make it turn out any better. And of course, every part of my life now – relationships, friends, etc. – is wonderful, not because I worked to make it that way, but because it unfolded that way through choosing my joy.

Finding Clarity in Times of Anxiety

Kim: Are there any tips that you could give people who experience anxiety with their awakening?

Jean: Yes. The first thing would be this: Just because you feel anxiety doesn't mean it's your guidance. You're going to feel anxiety now and then. It's part of being human and it comes with changes. You're going to feel fear, anxiety and discomfort: Physical, mental, emotional and spiritual discomfort. It happens – but it's not your guidance. So many people get scared or feel anxiety and then they pull back. They use those things to guide them, and that's not what they're for. Your real guidance is 'what you really want'. So many people say: "I really want this, but what if that happens? I don't know how to do it. Where will the money come from?" They talk themselves out of it. 'What I really want' is the guidance, and all this other stuff is going to come up anyway. Understand that it comes up, but don't give it too much weight in your life. Don't pay too much attention to it.

The second thing is this: Understand that all of that fear and anxiety, especially the fear of change, comes from aspects. It comes from some part of you that remembers when things went wrong, whether in this lifetime or another. You have many aspects, and they remember everything that ever went wrong or could go wrong, but it's their fear, it's not yours; your soul has no fear. Your soul has inspiration and joy and it pulls or invites you in the direction that's ultimately going to be most wonderful for you. And then your aspects bring up all this distraction. My advice would be to understand the difference between guidance and reactions from aspects, and make a very conscious choice as to what you pay attention to, what you "obey". It's all going to be there – excitement, joy, fear, worry, passion, anxiety – and it's up to you to decide what to follow: the guidance or the distractions, the joy or the fear.

Pearls of Wisdom

Kim: What is the one greatest thing that you've learned in all these years?

Jean: *That I'm okay, as is.* For so many reasons, in so many ways, that is not taught or learned in our society. From the moment you're born, to one degree or another, you learn that you're too loud or too quiet or too something; that you're just not okay as you are. Especially as a woman, and simply as a human being, there is lack of acceptance, a lot of judgment and you learn to internalize it. Then you try to make yourself fit in and get it 'right', especially if you're like me and take everything so dang seriously. So you try really hard to get everything right, but, by default, that means you're already getting it wrong. The most amazing thing to realize is that I'm not wrong! I still have to remind myself that it's okay to want that, it's okay to not want this or it's okay to feel whatever I'm feeling; it doesn't mean anything about anything. I'm okay however I am. I've learned a lot of amazing things, but that might be the most important.

Kim: What are you passionate about right now?

Jean: Pretty much everything! The passion for my own realization brings such a poignancy and depth of feeling to every life event, because you start to realize that these milestones won't happen again. There's a sense that it's the last time: The last time I'll love someone, the last time I'll say farewell or whatever. It's not even sad; it's just so deep. Everything becomes so precious. My passion is myself and that flows out into every part of my life. It's not like I think about it all the time, but there is sweetness to everything, because innately I know I am in the final moments of a very long journey.

Feeling into Enlightenment

Kim: What do you feel will be after ascension?

Jean: I feel that in enlightenment life is all about *experience*. Already now so much is about simply experiencing life. My son and I went on a trip to South Carolina, and he was complaining about the crappy hotel and all that, and for me it was like: Well, it's just an experience. The heat and the humidity, the crappy hotel, all that is just an experience of the human. In realization, it's just about being fully in the experience. Just a couple of weeks ago, my boss, whom I respect and admire and love, got upset about something I had missed. In the past it would have devastated me, but he's human, he gets mad about stuff, as we all do, and this time it was like: Wow, what a rush of energy! Instead of taking it personally, I just said, "Okay, I'll take care of it". So you really experience how it's all just energy; you don't turn it into some huge drama, you don't internalize it. If somebody gets mad at you, it's just an experience.

The Meaning of Spirituality

Kim: Is there something else that you would like to share about spirituality and what it means to you?

Jean: For me, spirituality is my life. Even calling it 'spirituality' separates it, but for the sake of discussion it's easier to use a term like spirituality. Nothing is valuable to me unless it's practical, something I can apply in everyday life. I grew up in a very religious family and even as a child I would see people spouting theology, but then do the nastiest things in their life, and I knew it wasn't right. For me, it has to have practical value every day. It can't be a segment of my life, like going to church on Sunday and being a jerk the rest of the week. That never made sense to me. When I go to town or go shopping, I'll do conscious breathing. Sometimes I feel overwhelmed by the energies, and if I remember to breathe, it helps immediately. The state you're in can shift in a breath, when you breathe and radiate. It's not that you try to crowd out other energies; rather, it's like if you're a candle flame, all the incoming energies make your flame flicker, but if you're a blowtorch, the wind isn't going to affect it. So whatever worldly experience I'm in, whether meetings or grocery shopping or traveling or anything, I try to remember to breathe my own essence and my presence, and to open my feelings. It's important to me to practice what I preach; to either make it real or shut up. It boils down to integration of all the parts and pieces of myself, all the aspects, and that's not a one-time thing that can be managed or forced. It's an ongoing process. When emotions show up, like fear, doubt, anger at someone else, or any of this stuff that we think is ours and have a problem with, it's nearly always aspects coming up to be integrated. So what I do is just be with the emotion, let it be there, feel it, and breathe it in.

In the last ten years, I've had some terrifying moments financially, like the rent being due in two days and no money, no food, all these hopeless situations. There's so much fear and it's easy to panic, but I finally realized how important it is to just be with that fear, allow it, and breathe it in. We so often try to hold it away from us, but when you allow it to be, you're actually allowing an unintegrated aspect to come home, maybe one that's been causing havoc and keeping you in poverty. I've learned to simply be with what is in myself, to not try to fix my anger or frustration or anxiety, but allow myself to feel it, to embody it within me, for that's when the alchemy happens. That is true transformation, not just mental processing or forcing yourself to be different (which doesn't work anyway). It's hard to explain, but you *choose* to remember who you are. It may sound strange, but that has been one the most practical and transformational things I have done for myself, allowing the integration of the aspects that have been causing the problems. Be okay with whatever you're feeling; there is nothing you'll ever feel that needs to be fixed, and by simply allowing, the situation will find its resolution.

Time Traveling

Kim: If you went back to your younger self at the darkest moments of awakening, what would you say to her?

Jean: I've actually done that, several times in my life. When I first moved to Colorado, made that first big leap of faith, for about four years it was very, very difficult. Not only financially, but also because there had been some misunderstandings and slander that had been shared about me by a disgruntled acquaintance. Some really bad rumours were spread about me just before I moved, so I arrived to a rather unwelcoming situation. For a long time I felt quite victimized by that, and for several years things were very painful, in addition to being wonderful and amazing too. In the darkest days I would hear this voice inside: "Five years from now, none of this will matter.

Your life is going to be completely different, just hang in there." And believe it or not, five years or so later, there was a moment when I found myself going back to that younger self and telling her: "You wouldn't believe how amazing my life is now." It saved my life! Whether it was me encouraging myself that it would be better in five years, or whether it was me going back to tell that younger self, "look how much better my life is now", or both, it doesn't matter. It's all bound up together anyway. I've gone back to some of my darkest moments and said, "It will change". I have also gone back to myself as a little girl, who had such a dark childhood in some ways, simply to love her and comfort her. I'd just hold her, and say "You're okay exactly as you are". There isn't one specific thing you need to say, but go back to those dark moments, feel what parts of you are calling out for help or reassurance, breathe yourself right there, and remind that self that it's going to be okay. And then it is, because you create it for yourself in that moment.

And it doesn't have to be only in the past. If life is difficult right now, invite your future self to come in and share that it gets better, because then you'll create it. In a way, it's like throwing an anchor out into the future and then pulling yourself towards it. You can anchor yourself in the 'oh, this is terrible' potential or in the 'oh, this is wonderful' potential. You set that point in your future and it draws you in. In fact, that's how you create your life!

Imagine: Five years from now, or one year from now, life will be different. You don't need to know the details, you don't have to set a goal for what should change. You simply choose that you're going to create something completely amazing for yourself. Then hold that knowing, and it will draw you toward that reality.

Conrado Sotomaior Justus de Souza Machado

Conrado was born in 1987 and is currently practicing and teaching law in Iguaçu Falls - Brazil, where he lives with his beloved mother and sister, who are also allowing their enlightenment. His father, who is a great man, lives nearby with his stepmother and two more sisters, who all have a special place in his heart. Conrado has a passion for enlightenment and teaching, loves to travel and is a big fan of deep breathing as a way of integrating self. Moreover, he is in a relationship with a very special and beautiful angel with whom he feels it has been a great pleasure to share love and the divine-human journey.

Life Before Awakening

Kim: Could you share your experience of the dark night of the soul?

Conrado: What happened for me was that I was very different before my awakening, like many of us. I was very entrenched in the ego and the sexual energy virus[17]. My childhood wasn't very traumatic, but I had a tendency to be a rebel and fight authority, and had problems at home. Later on I discovered that I carried anger and frustration towards religions from past lifetimes, so in this lifetime I wanted to stay out of any religious biases. I was more of an atheist and didn't really believe in God or in any spiritual belief systems.

---

17 A term used by the ascended master Tobias to describe a "consciousness virus", the root of the imbalance between the feminine and masculine energies as they have grown more and more separate over time.

I used to play with the dark energies, not in a magical or spiritual sense, but I listened to heavy metal and black metal. It can be enticing to play with these kinds of energies; it can give you a feeling of power. I became aggressive during my adolescence; I fought a lot at school and later on at parties. I also liked to be with many girls, and began to play with many types of drugs. First it was marihuana, then heavier drugs like cocaine, ecstasy, LSD. I began going to raves. So I became very imbalanced back then. I started going to the gym to become really strong and muscular, and my ego also became inflated. It was a very twisted energy. My mother said I was becoming a bit of a psycho but I didn't realize it at the time. So this was how my life was before.

Then what happened was that my mother started awakening and began to read channellings. She was the one to awaken first in our family and began to teach me some things. I believe that her awakening began to soften the energies at home. It was affecting me. When she talked to me about these spiritual things I felt a kind of nervousness, I didn't really want to hear it at the time and rejected most of it. But some things were slipping through…

Then I went to a workshop of Celia Fenn, and during the workshop, I felt something spinning in my head, and I fell asleep (while sitting) in the middle of the event. This was something that would never happen to me in another situation. So I began to get curious and started reading more channellings. Even though I began to see that there's some truth to it, I didn't have the motivation to let go of the old. I wasn't willing to fully enter this new world, because I had pleasure and at the time that was the best I knew. I didn't quite realize the implications of integration and of getting balanced. I didn't know that I would feel better than when being high on drugs. Now I know that even sex changes with Aliyah[18]: Now I have experiences with Aliyah that are more intense than I would have through regular sex with a girl. I couldn't see this coming at the time. So I resisted any real change until I got to a point when my dark night of the soul began.

Dark Night of the Soul

It was 2009: I was in law school, I was in a relationship and I also played in the local American football team. That November, in one week a series of events happened: First, I had an argument with a teacher at my college. Even though it wasn't a big deal, it was the beginning of an inner shift; energies began to stir up within me. Then, in the weekend, I travelled to another city to play a championship with my football team and had an argument with the team. When we got back home, my girlfriend told me she wanted to break up with me. It was a huge trigger at the time for me. I was having a lot of trouble in many areas of my life. When I was seeking comfort from her, she wanted to break up. So even though I wasn't really happy with the relationship, everything came up. A lot of rejection feelings. It felt really intense. This was the beginning of my dark night of the soul.

Before that I was really shut down to my feelings and emotions, I carried very imbalanced masculine energy and was deeply entrenched in the mind. Even sex and the fantasies came from a

18 The practice of physical self-love as presented by Tobias in the Sexual Energies School.

mental space, because even when some of these fantasies were realized, it didn't feel fulfilling. I can really perceive now that the fantasy was much bigger than the realization of it. I was very mental and shut down, always intelligent and using my mind: I was a chess player, and it was easy for me to pass exams at law school. I was really seeking pleasure, because there wasn't much feeling in my life. Only when I had emotional explosions from fighting or after taking drugs, I would feel something. It was still imbalanced emotions, rather than pure feelings. It's clear to me now how me being shut down to my feelings led to me becoming more imbalanced and always seeking for more and more pleasure. When you have a mental fantasy and realize it, but it doesn't fulfil you, then your mind gets more twisted and creates an even bigger fantasy. I was trapped in this wheel.

However, after these triggers that November, I couldn't keep the emotions shut down anymore, so everything came up at once. That happened also because I was already starting to become more aware. I knew that I couldn't deal with the situation in the same way as in the past. I knew that I had to change. That was really my motivation to let go of the old patterns, and to not let my mind dictate what I wanted to do.

From that moment on, I began to read all the Crimson Circle materials from the first channel to the last one, reading a lot every day. I really began to dive into myself, to integrate and release those emotions that came to the surface. It was really intense. I had times when I would scream alone, punch pillows or the wall because of all the anger from the past that was coming up all at once. But I didn't do things like I had done in the past like smash people's cars with a baseball bat or this kind of thing. I would just stay at home, go a bit to the office. I stopped going to parties. I would just stay at home breathing and releasing, breathing and releasing. I would cry a lot.

This was the beginning of my shift. Since then I've never really stopped listening to channels and doing conscious breathing, always keeping my focus on my ascension, my integration. I felt that this is what I really want, what will bring me the fulfilment; this is what will bring me the freedom to create what I want, the freedom to share experiences with other people on a deeper level without attachment and energy feeding. During this intense process I really got a feeling about what ascension is; I believe that part of the work that the ascended masters do, is showing us what is possible, showing us different states of consciousness. When you know that it is possible, it's a lot easier to not lose your focus anymore.

Living in Mastery

Kim: How do you experience your life now?

Conrado: Something that helped me stay focused at first was that I had no choice. The emotions were too intense and if I tried to escape them in the old ways, it got worse. So I dived deeper into the process (of awakening). I noticed, that if you really want to go through this process fast, *you can*. Not through struggle or force, but through staying on track: Breathing, listening, and living what you have learned. When you stay very focused, the changes can start to happen really fast for you.

Before my awakening, I wasn't really a traveller. But since my awakening, I wanted to start participating in workshops. I started to travel a lot: I would just make a choice, and then I'd be there. It was a really big shift for me. Then I began to get really involved with this work, and discovered that I love to attend and to help organising events. My friendships changed very fast: I lost contact with old friends and started to make friends with people who are also in their awakening process. My mother started hosting meetings at our house for friends, where we would read the materials. She would talk and guide the breathing, and later I also started doing that. My life really changed, because the energy dynamics changed. These new relationships and the consciousness work is a big part of my life now. How I relate to people is much more open, I stay in my centre, and have a new sense of self.

I'm still in law practice, but it's different now because it doesn't cause as much stress anymore. It can still be challenging, and sometimes I face resistance towards the law practice; a part of me feels that these things are boring. This is one of the areas that I'm still integrating, where aspects still show up. However, I also feel that my current situation is serving a purpose: I always felt that I had a natural ability to be a teacher. But at the same time, I had a big fear of public speaking. I've been integrating that aspect, and then my mother invited me to teach at the law school. The night before my first teaching day, I couldn't sleep and my energy was really stuck. Now I'm an environmental law teacher. In some aspects my life didn't change very much yet, but I feel that in many ways, these experiences have served as a preparation. I couldn't really be a good teacher in the future with a fear of public speaking. I feel that when these aspects are integrated, more changes will come.

Kim: How do you find a balance between focusing on spirituality and working in the (often very mental) academic world?

Conrado: There comes a point when you might not be teaching people about spiritual things or do spiritual work, but you stay in a point of presence, and you just relate to people in a different way, in a lighter way. You reach a point where you feel okay with yourself and with what you have chosen to do at the moment. At that point it doesn't really matter what topic you are teaching, it's just an experience, an interaction with the students. Of course, it's not the same thing as teaching something spiritual, but the fact that I'm teaching law doesn't really affect me anymore. In the end, it's just about conveying some information while you are relating to the students. Sometimes I talk to the students, tell jokes and so on. The subject is just the surface-layer of the teaching experience, and there are so many other layers present. For example, you, as a teacher, can stay in your centre, and that in itself shows something to others. That's what really matters; how you are feeling inside, how you are relating to people, how conscious you are. So you get to a point where the subject matter doesn't matter, where winning cases, or telling people what's right and what's wrong doesn't matter, because you realize it's all about choice. Your perspective changes, and you realize that every experience is about what the person is consciously or unconsciously creating.

Kim: What a relief to come to that point where you are so deeply at peace with yourself that what you do doesn't matter much.

Conrado: Yes, and nevertheless, I feel that the more you are in that state of being at peace with yourself, the more your life starts to flow in a new direction. The more I expand, the more my experiences will expand with me. For me, teaching at Law School is part of the process, and I know it's a phase that won't last forever.

Kim: What do you do on a daily basis to keep your focus and balance?

Conrado: I invite my soul to breathe with me many times a day, I make a conscious choice to live, and to stay in my body. I practice staying present, to stop thinking so much. When I am talking to other people, I focus on not letting my mind take me away from my centre, to not get involved in other people's mental stream. Often people who are not so awakened, (unconsciously) want you to go along with their mental stream, so they can take your energy, exchange energy with you but in an imbalanced way. I'm always practicing giving full attention to people, to really listen to them from my centre, so that we can relate on other levels (rather than on a mental level). I try to not get involved in energy stealing. I do Aliyah every week like Tobias recommends; I take a few Sundays every month to do nothing, during which I disconnect from computers, the Internet and phones, and just stay with myself and breathe, allowing the integration. I pay attention to my dreams (at night). They can really show what's going on on other levels: what aspects are on the surface, if you are imbalanced, your future potentials... What is also important is to always practice non-reactivity: To not react when other people attack me or are emotional; I always try to stay in my centre, to not judge and not let my emotional aspects react. During these moments, the best thing you can do is to not say anything, not react internally but just stay present; let the energies flow, just let it pass as the person goes through their process.

Distilled Wisdom

Kim: What is the greatest thing you have learned through your awakening?

Conrado: Loving yourself. It may sound like a cliché, but it's not. It's really very important, because it's not possible to have these kinds of interactions that we are having, interactions on a deeper level, if you didn't start to love and accept yourself. And if you do, this is what makes integration possible, what really wakes you up. When you allow that love, or compassion, to start flowing into your life, you feel fulfilled. For me the Sexual Energies School[19] was really important, because it's one of the fastest ways of releasing the stuck energies that prevent you from loving yourself.

Time Traveling

Kim: If you were to meet your younger self again, or someone who was struggling with that inner void, what would you say to them?

Conrado: Probably not much. I feel that it's more about sharing the moment, being a reflection of what's possible, and just being there for the other person. So they can feel that this experience can be safe, that there is someone who lives in this space. So they can sense this peacefulness that comes with the safe space and with the knowingness that you are God also. What was also important for me to realize was that we do create everything in our reality; it's all about taking full responsibility.

---

19   You can read more about this course here: www.crimsoncircle.com/ Events/Advanced-Studies/Advanced-Studies-Classes/Sexual-Energies

Anne Maribo Andersen and Finn Andersen

Anne and Finn met in 1971, and have 2 sons. Both school teachers, they have worked with kids of many ages in public and private schools. Since 1979, both have given sessions in massage, healing and later in art therapy, aura-soma (Anne) and voice, toning (Finn).

They started participating in the Crimson Circle in 2001 and later became Certified Crimson Circle Teachers and Mentor Teachers. In 2014 Anne and Finn received the *Inspire Consciousness Award* from the Crimson Circle. In the same year, they started *Consciousness Theater for Kids*. The purpose is to teach children how to stop their victim (or bully) roles, letting go of power games, and how to like/love themselves. The tools used in these workshops that have been taught in school classes, are role-playing (by Anne and Finn), breathing, grounding etc.

Now Finn and Anne mostly offer teacher trainings of this material, and enjoy their creativity through painting and writing children's books (Anne) and music (Finn) and also by creating a garden of joy and beauty together.

The Beginning

Kim: How did your awakening begin?

Anne: My very first spiritual experience was when I was fourteen, at my confirmation ceremony. After this ritual ended, we had communion with the bread and wine and in that moment at the altar, I saw the figure of Jesus, as light, and I was shivering all over. That was where it started for me. I have always been interested in what is behind the surface of things. Five years after Finn and I met in 1971, we joined a commune where we lived together with a group of adults and children. Each evening we were doing psychodrama together, where each person individually went to the middle of the group to express something. The point was to express your emotions in a kind of creative way, creating something from it. That was a rather cool experience and the basis of some of the things we are doing now in our Consciousness Theater for Kids -work. A lot of what we did back then was uncovering the unconscious stuff. All the stories about what your parents have done to you, how bad it was and so on... (laughing)

After that it became more of a spiritual search through massage and healing. Massage was for me a good way to get grounded and to start using my senses. It was a kind of intuitive massage. That was part of opening up, but the real turning point for me was when I met the Crimson Circle through our dentist, who asked if we had heard about Kryon. In 2001, we got a transcript of a channel from Tobias (of the Crimson Council) and it was for me the feeling of coming home. The way you look at things in a lot of other spiritual groups that I have come across was that you have to become a better human, or that the human has no significance – it's all about spirit.

Finn: I feel that I have had some accidents in my life where I stumbled, and realized something while I was down. The first was when I was 10 years old and fell two meters down the stairs into the cellar with a bucket of coal over my head.

I went into hospital and realized that I could see myself in that accident from the outside. I had a similar experience at 19, when a car drove into me while I was on a bicycle: I fell down and hit my head once again. This time I could see myself from above, I could see how the man who had driven into me took his military cap off and put it between my teeth; I saw everything that was going on.

And then Anne and I have gone through the same courses and classes and have followed this process together. It has been very enriching, also in regards to our relationship. When we moved together and later had children, I didn't know how to express my aggression or anger when I was not satisfied with something – I didn't want to scold. So instead of talking with Anne when I was angry with her, I would leave the house and slam the door and then take a long walk. I did not want to use my fists as my father had done towards my mother. So it took a long time for me to learn how to express my anger.

Learning to Express Anger

Kim: How did you learn to express anger in a more balanced way?

Anne: I also feel that in my family, kids were not allowed to express anger, only my father was allowed to do that. So, when you feel as a child that something is not okay but you are not allowed to express that, you keep a lot of things inside of you. When I was young and started going to parties, this anger came out when I was drunk. It was not very constructive at all. But the psychodrama was helpful: It showed me that it's okay to have these emotions and let them out in a creative way so that they can be released, rather than explode when this inner tension becomes too much.

I have always done painting, and to me that has been a great help for expressing myself without words. This helps you to not think too much but stay with your feelings and emotions. I also had a lot of depression during my awakening, and painting was a way out of it. It showed myself what is going on and what is behind the surface. Painting is also a great joy.

These days I express my anger in a calmer way. It's also about not compromising my boundaries. Some things are okay and some things are not. If it's not okay, you have to say "no" or express how you feel about it. You don't have to be emotional, you can just say, "No way! This doesn't work for me."

Finn: One of the things that I have learned about aggression is that it is just one of the ways of expressing something. Aggression is needed in communication, so that your message is understood clearly. As I have become more aware, my walk has become shorter and shorter, so that today it is perhaps seconds rather than an hour, because I express what I feel.

Sharing the Experience of Awakening

Kim: What has it been like to go through awakening together with your partner?

Anne: For me it has been such a great thing to be able to share experiences; that when you have experienced something deep within, you can share that with the person who means the most to you. We have some friends where only the woman is Shaumbra. When both of you are doing the same things (spiritually), you are much more open and you can see what the other person is doing, and your partner can see your patterns. But to me it would be like missing something if we couldn't share these deep things. You can never say this is the only right way. But I know many friends who left their husband at some point because there were too many differences between how they perceived the world, their lives and the relationship.

That's one of the other things; you have to be aware that the energy exchange between the two of you is balanced. Of course, it wasn't like that for us in the beginning when we met. I was often very depressed, and that is also one of these feeding games. Probably that is also why we are good at teaching about consciousness to kids because we have gone through all this stuff from the inside. When you are aware of what is really going on, you can also hold some distance to what is happening and even make fun of the situation.

Kim: How has your relationship changed?

Anne: When something happens, when I feel that he has crossed my boundary, we talk about it together (after taking a few deep breaths). We talk about both of our patterns. It's always the case that they are somehow connected. I feel that we are supporting each other in getting more clarity and in letting go of these patterns. And of course, it's also an inner work, looking at yourself.

Finn: One thing I have been aware of is that when you are a couple, you also have a responsibility in how you act towards other people together. It's necessary to be aware of this common energy. Kahlil Gibran, in *the Prophet*, expresses it very beautifully: You are like two trees with a common crown, but you stand on your own roots. When you are two, there is also a third energy that is common and shared. That's why I feel we have so much energy in our projects that we do together.

Kim: What does a conscious relationship look like in practice?

Finn: One thing is that when you are not involved in these energy-feeding games, a lot of energy is freed to do what you really want to do. You do not waste a lot of time on drama.

Anne: What I also find important is that we're not together all the time. Especially I need this, having grown up as an only child. We have a house where we can be in separate rooms, and be by ourselves when one of us needs to do that. The other thing is that we are working together with our projects. I find that is a way of taking all the experiences of our lives and of our awakening, all the things that we have learned and transforming that into something new, something that is our creation.

In our daily life, we have divided the chores at home so we don't have to discuss who does what. We have an agreement, and we sometimes ask the other person to help or to switch over if we want.

Finn: For me it is all about freedom: feeling free and being free. Talking about how to feel free, how we can do things in a way that is best for both of us.

Anne: I think it's also very important in a relationship to be able to support each other in a good way. To see through the layers, to see the other person's soul. Of course, you can do that with everybody, but if you want to live together with someone for some time, it's important to have this connection soul to soul, and not just the physical, earthly journey.

Kim: Sovereign, yet intimate relationships – is that possible?

Finn: That is where the most work has to be done: To be clear about how you would like things to be in the relationship. You have to find agreement with your partner. It's about saying this is how I feel and what I need, and then it's up to the other person to say yes or no. Do I choose the relationship or not? It's a point of choice that is on-going. Just like in life you have to constantly choose what is right for you. It's actually very simple.

Anne: It's mostly about going within, and feeling "what would I like to do?" If something that is really important to me couldn't happen in my relationship, then I would surely leave. It's important to listen to yourself. For example, sometimes one of us needs to sleep by himself/herself. So if you feel within yourself and have this desire or need, you should do it and not compromise yourself. I feel that's what we are doing. Having respect for the other, and allowing yourself first, to choose what you want. I don't feel we have conflicts with that anymore.

Finn: No, I don't either.

Anne: I really have this feeling that our relationship was an agreement made on the other side, perhaps also karmic, but at some point, we released the karma and chose something new so that we could really support each other by doing this journey together. At the same time, this journey is something very individual.

Through and Beyond Challenges

Kim: Could you talk about some of the more challenging aspects of your journey?

Anne: Part of the journey has been to get another relationship to my parents. My dad passed away quite early, but my mom, she has really been one of these "challenges". Wanting to keep control of me, that has also been quite a journey. I've found that we came to a certain understanding. In her last 1,5 years she was sent to a home for elderly people, quite close to where we live. That was nice to be able to meet with her in a clearer way for the last 1,5 years. At the same time, it was also a relief when she died, because it was tough in a way to meet with her. She could do very little by herself and was longing after her old more active life. And of course, nobody could help her with that.

Finn: What I found that you were good at, Anne, was to set your boundaries with your mother: If you did not feel that something was right, you would tell her, and that is surely one of those things that most people have difficulty with (namely to set boundaries to their parents).

Anne: Yes, because it's ingrained in you, this relationship is more unconscious than other relationships that you have later on in life because you were born into it.

What has been a challenge for us for quite some years is the whole abundance issue. It's this old pattern, this suffering

274

game. It has been quite a lot of work to let go of that. I feel it's rather balanced now. And I also feel it has much to do with loving yourself and feeling that you are worthy of the good things in life. Well, that also includes having physical abundance for the human needs. There were many times when we had no money, but strangely enough, when there was some course or spiritual event that we really wanted to participate in, somehow we always got the money, one way or another. Actually the important part is not how much money you have but that you have this trust that when there is something that you need, it will be there.

What I have used when things were tough, besides painting, is being in nature. Taking long walks, mostly by myself. It's kind of a thing that when you walk, you ground yourself. It's also nurturing, and it gives you this feeling that you'll get through it somehow. I don't know other things that can really do that. Another great thing has been to meet other like-minded people. Actually our friends have always been people who have also taken this journey. I don't think we have had many so-called normal friends, only family, our two sons and their families. Other family members we see once or twice a year at most.

The Gift of Self-Expression

Kim: How has self-expression and creativity served you?

Anne: There is such a joy in expressing yourself, expressing from our inner depth, expressing what is me, exploring what do I really want to express, having the courage to step out of the normal. I also have another project that has been on standstill for a while. To write a children's book. My purpose with that is to show the kids that there is more than one reality, more than just this physical reality; that there are also things going on in other dimensions. So-called "good" things and also tough things.

Finn: Along the way I have also used the tool of working with music and with the voice, to understand what is happening. The connection between sound and body, and how you can create a balanced energy with that. Now I am retired, but I still give some music classes from time to time just for fun. (I gave music lessons at the Danish public school for 20 or 30 years). I have a feeling of connection with the children, it is as if they do not reflect so much of their irritation on me because I feel this connection with them, and they feel that I am there. So they can share and also receive some of what I have to share. I have also used my voice my whole life and played different instruments, so I can share my joy for music with other people.

Definitions of Enlightenment

Kim: What does enlightenment mean for you?

Anne: It has surely been the goal for this lifetime. So I just know, it happens at some point and it's enough to just relax and allow.

Finn: I do not think so much about it. I have the same feeling as Anne regarding that this is the last lifetime. I have more clarity and joy in my life than there has ever been before. So, it's as if I am integrating what you call enlightenment into my presence and into the here and now. Not something that is lying ahead, or that I will cross over at some point. It's like the more I am in my presence and feeling joy right here and now, the more I am getting there.

Anne: I've come to think of this as being the master. When you can be in your mastery, it's being in the whole acceptance of everything in your life. I'm not quite there yet. I feel like the more you can see life from the master-perspective, the easier life is, and the more fun.

Time Traveling

Kim: What would you say to your younger self who is struggling through awakening?

Anne: It will all work out, just enjoy it. You'll get through it.

Finn: Just be happy.

Anne: Listen to yourself. Allow yourself to feel. Be in nature!

Finn: Do what feels right for you.

Anne: Often in the beginning of the awakening there is a feeling of being different from others, and that can be tough. Others think you are really crazy, having such strange ideas. So just listen to yourself and keep being true to yourself.

Finn: What we also talk about to the children is that what you pay attention to will grow. Choose what you want to pay attention to. I think that is rather important.

Anne: I would like to add something to that: It's not about

suppressing things that are uncomfortable. It's like, okay they are there, but it's not your main focus. I think that's a problem when people use things like positive affirmations, they kind of suppress the other stuff. Everything is allowed to be there, but you can choose where to put your focus. And of course, when you are in the middle of your awakening it's often so tough. Especially if you are doing it really alone, without having friends with whom you can talk about it.

Finn: Ask yourself: What do I need right now? - and then give it to yourself.

Part 5

Distilled Wisdom

Spiritual First Aid

Below you can find several pages of short, easy actions or insights that you can apply to any situation that causes you anxiety or imbalance. They are tailored specifically for the awakening human. There is no order or hierarchy to these different tools; instead you can choose either randomly or intuitively 1-3 of these items and apply them to your current situation. The awakening path rarely follows patterns, and something that might have worked yesterday might not work today. The list includes enough different items to ensure that there's something for every situation related to awakening anxiety. Some of these items are actions, and others are reminders to help you shift your perspective, but in essence they are all about spiritual self-care.

Another effective way to use this list is to go through it from top to bottom, focusing on each item intensively for a week. This is awakening in action. All of these tools are about practical spirituality, about applied and embodied consciousness. Moreover, these tools do not require a lot of time, nor do they require money or commitment to a specific spiritual tradition or discipline. They are tools to support the modern, sovereign human on the path to self-actualization.

♠ *Anchor Yourself*: Consciously and consistently ground yourself by feeling your body, feeling your feet against the ground and by choosing to be present here on Earth, here at this time, here in this body. Whereas the mind has the tendency to regret the past and to worry about the future, the body is always in the now-moment. The more you expand into other dimensions, the more important it is to anchor yourself into this point of presence. A great way of grounding yourself is by *toning*, since using your voice consciously brings you into awareness of your body in the now moment.

♠ *Allow the Experience*: I like to take a moment of 'allowing' each morning – allowing the energies to flow without me trying to do anything. What if you allowed yourself, for just a moment each day, to forget about your human identity, forget about all the things you have done, or will do or should do, and simply allowed yourself to *be*? For inspiration, study the behaviour of cats, who are masters at allowing. Although you can be in a state of allowing at any time in any place, some people find music helpful. Yin yoga is one way to practice allowing.

♠ *Go Beyond Time and Space*: Feel time and space moving through you. Let go of holding on to time and space, until nothing is here except the presence of the present moment. Feel that time and space are not a cage that limits you, but just variables shifting in and out of your reality, and that you are the point of presence, you are the one constant element in your life. You are peace itself, and anything you need will come to you in the right moment. You can also try this experience: Imagine that your memory was wiped and you didn't remember anything about your previous life. How would you act in this moment? When we release our attachments to past events, our past identity and our perceptions about past events, we experience the self purely in the present moment. Conversely, the more we experience ourselves consciously in the present moment, the more our attachments to the past dissolve. The more we release our attachments to the past, the easier it is to release any anxiety concerning the future.

♠ *Press Pause*: When those emotions feel overwhelming and you feel the urge to react to something or someone, take a step back, a *time-out*. Hit pause, and take a moment to simply observe, feel and breathe. Allow the breath to do its magic and move the emotional or mental energies that have become stuck or entangled. Even if you're in the middle of a conversation, it's better to leave the room and take a pause for breathing than to lash out and say something that you can't unsay afterwards. There is always enough time for a conscious breath.

♠ *Shake It Off*: Moving your body in any way that feels enjoyable is so important for releasing stuck energies and for cleansing the mind. Find out how you like to move your body, whether it's swimming, walking, yoga or shaking your hips to your favourite music. The body actually releases trauma by shaking, so if you feel your body spontaneously shaking or shivering, let it shake.

♠ *Release, Release, Release*: Disconnect from everything that is not yours. As an awakened human, you'll come to realize that what you want and need tends to be very different from what your ego expected you to need and want. The more you dare to release that which is naturally dying within you, the more you will discover what truly serves you. You can release anything that feels constricting, disempowering, or not in alignment with who you choose to be in this moment. You can release something without abolishing it from your life. Releasing something simply means that it no longer has control over you.

♠ *Choose the Safe Space*: Every day, and particularly when you go to sleep and when you feel anxious or overwhelmed, choose the safe space. The safe space is not a space devoid of pain, hurt, or even fear; it is a space where all feelings are allowed without judgement. When fear is allowed without resistance, it quickly transforms into peace. Choosing the safe space means allowing the presence of soul to coexist with the human in all its imperfection and vulnerability.

♠ *Take Responsibility*: Despite the fact that you can't control the world around you or other people, and you can't even control your own feelings, you are a divine creator and you can create new situations, new solutions, and new answers. Start where you are, using whatever resources you have. Taking responsibility is a gift from you to yourself and it can be taken without a dose of judgement.

♠ *Energy Seeks Resolution – Naturally*: Did you know that you don't need to manipulate your energy field to rebalance? Energies flow naturally, and energy always seeks resolution. Your job is to relax yourself enough to allow the walls of resistance to melt. Whatever you need comes to you the moment you stop trying to manipulate energies.

Try this metaphysical experiment: Let's say you are in a state of anxiety. Your mind is full of worries and you can't concentrate on anything else. Start feeling your body: Where can you feel tension, pain, heaviness or numbness? Perhaps you feel as if there was a knot in your stomach. This is an example of stuck energy in your system. The good news is that this energy will organically start to flow the minute you allow it to. So, without trying to change or manipulate or fix that knot in your stomach, simply feel it and start breathing slowly, inhaling through the nose. Make a choice to *allow* the energies to move *when they are ready to*. Then continue breathing until you feel the knot unknotting. As you do this process, you might notice emotions rising to the surface. Allow any emotions, thoughts or sensations to simply flow through you. When the energies flow again, it will be much easier to solve the problem on a practical and physical level. Notice any changes that take place in the upcoming days or weeks.

♠ *Receive Love From Soul*: Talk to your soul/inner master. Start a conscious relationship with your soul. Feel yourself as your soul. See yourself through the eyes of your soul. Ask soul for a gift. Ask soul to teach you how to receive love, how to trust yourself and how to feel her/his presence. Feel how there is no separation between your human self and your eternal wise self.

♠ *You Are Never Stuck*: When we are in an unwanted situation, it often feels like we are imprisoned by circumstances and by our own negativity. Yet everything is so flexible in this universe, if we allow it. Your body is a mass of constantly changing, moving particles – you are not a constant being. At times, it's hard to believe that reality is not a fixed thing, because you can't actually *see* the movement of the atoms with your bare eyes. It's hard to believe, but freedom really is just a step away from anywhere. Take a small step towards relief, and then take another; because no matter how heavy or dark your feeling-state is now, you can shift it and it doesn't have to take effort.

If you are in a dark place, it might take a bit of time before you can feel overflowing love, joy, or gratitude. But it just takes one step to feel a bit lighter. To feel some relief, to feel the air in your lungs, to feel a thread of life flowing through you. The only reason why we fear being in any situation is because we believe that we are stuck in it. Once you realize this is just a belief that you can cast out of the window, you are *never* stuck.

♠   *Allow Joy*: Joy is a way of sensing and experiencing life, and unlike happiness, which is usually artificial and temporary, joy is the ever-present undercurrent pleasure of beingness experienced by soul. Instead of trying to replace sadness and boredom with joy, consider viewing joy as an additional flavour to life, something that always exists alongside the human emotions. When I was integrating my stage fright, I discovered that the most effective way to deal with that fear is joy: When I focused on the pure joy of acting and expressing myself, the fear slowly melted away. Joy is the natural state of the soul, and it is always available, no matter what experiences your human self is going through.

♠   *Don't Hurry or Force Anything*: Just because the majority of people in the Western world are obsessed with living busy, stressful, neurotic lives, doesn't mean there is any good reason for hurrying through life. Indulge in each moment, and listen to the rhythm of your soul. Everything flows more gracefully when we don't force anything, not even awakening, but follow the flow.

♠   *Enjoy Your Sensuality*: Enjoying your senses is one of the fastest way to transcend the limitations and obsessions of the mind. Spirituality and sensuality are not contradictions – the true nature of human spirituality is sensual. Perhaps you've learned that sensuality is somehow not pure. This, of course, is nothing but mass hypnosis created a long time ago by religious organizations whom it benefited to have people feeling ashamed of their sensuality. Embodied mastery is the sensual experience of divinity, which is then expressed through creation and celebration. Sensuality means *feeling your experience* without resistance. Therefore, feel with all of your senses, feel with an open heart and even feel with your imagination.

♠   *Water It Down*: Drink water, bathe in it, swim in it, stare at the ocean, drown your sorrows in it... Water cleanses and rebalances your body and mind and neutralizes harsh energies. Don't underestimate the importance of water, especially as you go through transformations.

♠   *Pamper Your Human Self*: Awakening is tough. Treat yourself as kindly and luxuriously as possible in all situations.

♠   *Self-Expression*: Turn experiences into expressions, and they transform from pain and worthlessness into beauty and meaning. Self-expression doesn't have to be artistic, it could simply mean saying out loud how you feel about something, buying flowers to decorate your home, or choosing something special to wear just for the fun of it. When in doubt, wear red lipstick! Or whatever the equivalent is for men.

♠   *Sense the Beauty*: Sometimes everything can feel wrong, but that doesn't mean there is no purpose to that experience. Beauty is one of those purposes and can heal a broken heart or save a bad day. Play a game of noticing anything around you that you find beautiful. Bask in beauty, breathe it in, acknowledge it and create more of it. Being able to appreciate beauty is a strength, an asset that can support you remarkably on this journey.

♠   *Celebrate*: Celebration is the art of life. Celebrate life, celebrate death, celebrate your achievements, or celebrate the phase of the moon… Celebrate something, anything, at least once a day.

♠   *Allow the Expansion*: We have a tendency to hide and suffocate any uncomfortable feelings, which only makes them more persistent. However, if you allow those emotions to breathe and to expand, they become much lighter. Your soul is expansive enough to accommodate all your feelings and all of your aspects. Expansion doesn't have to be metaphysical; you can do it on a physical level, if you prefer: Stretch your arms wide, open your chest, roll your shoulders back, inhale deeply and lift your chin – that's expanding your energies! Can you feel the difference? The more you allow your energies to expand, the more you can enjoy the expansion of your awareness (that's all awakening really is).

♠   *Imagine*… Imagination is the doorway to multi-dimensionality. Imagination frees you from the patterns, limitations, and greyness of everyday life. Imagination also allows new potentials to flow into your life. If you are out of practice, read a novel that entices you and allow your imagination to participate deeply and sensually. You can also spend some time with your inner child, or do some intentional daydreaming.

♠   *Journaling*: Keeping a journal of your feelings and insights (and dreams, if you like) is so enriching: It leaves a record of your experiences and allows you to see certain patterns that you might otherwise have missed. Journaling helps you to ground any insights that you've gained, and on a bad day it reminds you of your own wisdom. In addition, it strengthens the connection to your inner master and allows you to express and alchemize difficult emotions. If you're not into journaling about your feelings, try anyway by writing bullet points, short notes, poems, quotes or song lyrics, or by drawing.

♠   *Don't Compromise Your Boundaries*: Be aware of your boundaries and communicate them clearly. The more grounded and present you are in your body, the less other people's energies will affect you negatively. In order to keep your boundaries, you also need to find out what you like, need, don't like, don't accept and so on. The more you practice, the easier it will get to stand up for your boundaries. Healthy boundaries always start with self-respect, and develop self-trust.

♠   *Accept Support*: Asking for help is not a weakness; it's necessary if you want to stay sane while going through the process of awakening. See yourself as the leader of a team: Like any good leader, you don't try to do everything by yourself, but you ask your family, friends, as well as angels and ascended masters to support you. Especially when you are not feeling safe (physically, emotionally, or in any other way), asking for help is empowering. Life is so much easier when there are at least a couple of people whom you trust and who can help you in difficult times. In addition, there are countless non-physical beings who are just waiting to support you. They are not there to replace your own wisdom, but merely to reflect back your mastery, and to remind you of that which you already know. When you communicate with beings who are not embodied, always start by first connecting to your own inner master. These beings communicate intuitively and multi-dimensionally, rarely through words. Here is my list of friends from beyond the veil who are always available when I need support and who specialize in helping humans who are awakening:

- *Saint-Germain* specializes in helping humans through the self-realization process. Call upon him whenever you need support with alchemizing energies or to discover more about true freedom.

- *Koot Hoomi lal Singh* can help you to get out of your mind in a safe and graceful way. He is also wonderful at inspiring humour and creativity. He spent around 20 years as an embodied human master after his ascension.

- *Kuan Yin* is the embodiment of compassion. Whenever you want to turn a harsh situation into softer energies, call upon Kuan Yin – no darkness is deep enough to scare her.

- *Maria (Merit) Magdalene* can help you to discover self-love and transmute any wounds of shame, guilt and trauma into freedom.

- *El Morya Khan* is a great support in clearing your energies and can help you to cut through illusion into clarity.

- *Archangel Raphael* is the expert of transmuting fear of any kind. He is also wonderful company when you are healing from a broken heart.

- *Archangel Amael* is the archangel of hope, and can help you move beyond despair into a new dawn.

♠ *Listen to Your Body*: Your body knows exactly what's best for you, whether it's more sleep, more fresh air or a different diet. And don't be surprised if those needs change often, even on a daily basis. Your body also communicates to you about your emotional state and about energy dynamics between you and others. If you suppress your body's messages for too long, it will start to speak to you through illness.

♠ *Authenticity*: It's okay to hide yourself from others, but the only way to feel authentically good is to be authentic with yourself. *What do you want in this moment?* What do you need right now? How can you enjoy your life right now? What would 'following your bliss' mean today?

♠ *Choose New*: Every day is different – can you trust yourself so deeply that you know you're safe even if every day is a new day? The truth of who you are keeps expanding. New requires courage, but sooner or later you will come to a point where you've simply had enough of the old. Be playful with the new, explore the new, be surprised by the new, create the new.

♠ *Be OK With Things Not Making Sense*: You can't understand or learn Spirit, but you can experience it. It's a lot like love: Analyse it, write about it, but when you've had enough of all that, just allow yourself to experience it. Life is becoming more and more unpredictable, so it's best to get used to things not making sense.

♠ *Let the Energies Serve You*: Act as if your job was to simply receive good things from life, and it will become so. Only someone who receives unconditionally can give unconditionally. Act as if every event in your life, every person that you encounter, is sent to you for your highest good. The more you start to embody this perspective, to act like this, the more you create this.

♠ *Honour Yourself, Honour Others*: So simple, yet it can make all the difference.

♠ *Take a Step – Into Any Direction*: When you feel stuck, just take one step into any direction, and the energies will start flowing, Master Kuthumi teaches. Literally taking a walk can also help you get out of your mind.

♠ *Spend Time in Nature*: Being in nature is rebalancing, rejuvenating and healing. Try also being in nature by yourself, in silence.

♠ *Consciously Distract Yourself*: When your mind gets overactive, or when you feel emotionally overwhelmed, it's OK to consciously distract yourself for a while: Watch a movie, invite your friends over, travel... Sometimes we get so serious with our awakening journey that the most effective way to shift through stuck energy is to take a short break from our own lives.

♠ *Don't Take Your(human)self Too Seriously*: Your human identity and personality is not all that you are, so don't take it too seriously. When that human self is screaming that everything is going wrong, remember that there are more important things in life than problems.

♠ *Keep Away From the Idiots*: Some people are trouble, and that's just how it is. As an adult, you have the choice to walk away from people who don't support your wellbeing. Life gets a lot easier when you learn to choose the right crowd. Remember also, that crowd may change as you change.

♠ *Don't Hold Back*: Energies are meant to flow freely. Don't resist that which comes to you, and don't hold back that which wants to flow through you. You are here on this planet to feel (in other words to receive) and to radiate (transmit) energies. You are the channel of your own soul; if your soul wants to create big or be expressive or sing out loud, then, for heaven's sake, don't stand in your own way!

♠ *Forgive Yourself*: Forgiving others and receiving forgiveness from others doesn't really free you unless you are ready to also forgive yourself (all of yourself!). Forgiving yourself completely and unconditionally is self-love at its purest, and one of the final steps to your realization.

♠ *All Is Well, You Exist*: When all hope is lost, remember that your eternal, creative essence always exists. Even if you are full of hope, remember that you always exist. This realization will carry you beyond the fear of death into the sensual, free experience of life.

♠ *Laugh!* When all else fails (and in the meantime), laugh.

* * *

I hope you have enjoyed the reading experience. Please consider writing a short review on your favourite retailer website. Thank you!

Resources and Recommendations

A short list of books and websites that support the awakening human (of course, there are tons of spiritual books and teachings available – I've listed here the ones that have helped me the most or that resonate with my perspective. Many of these materials are created for the modern and sovereign spiritual explorer and do not follow any particular spiritual tradition/lineage).

Books

Adamus Saint-Germain, channelled through Geoffrey and Linda Hoppe: *Memoirs of a Master*

Adamus Saint-Germain, channelled through Geoffrey and Linda Hoppe: *Live Your Divinity*

Eckhart Tolle: *A New Earth*

Eckhart Tolle: *The Power of Now*

Gary Lachman: *Madame Blavatsky – The Mother of modern Spirituality*

Gerhard Fankhauser: *Urfan - The Adventurous Journey to the secret Mystery School* (a novel)

Irvin Yalom: *Creatures of a Day*

Irvin Yalom: *Staring at the Sun*

Jonette Crowley: *The Eagle and the Condor*

Koot Hoomi channelled through Marisa Calvi: *Let's Go for a Walk – book series*

Koot Hoomi lal Singh and El Morya: *The Mahatma Letters to A. P. Sinnett*

Lauren Hutton: *Becoming Sar'h*, Book 1

Maria Szepes: *The Red Lion: The Elixir of Eternal Life* (a novel)

Maurice Kok: *The Journey of an Ascended Master Named Kiora Amo*

Paramhansa Yogananda: *Autobiography of a Yogi*

Rollo May: *The Courage to Create*

Teal Swan: *Shadows Before Dawn*

Teal Swan: *Sculptor of the Sky*

Verla Ell Rey: *The Age of Self: The Self as the Final Frontier*

Various authors: The Mahatma Letters

Websites

Eckhart Tolle: www.eckharttolle.com (videos focusing on being present and transcending the limitations of the mind.)

Jean Tinder: www.youaregodalso.com/creator-cards/ (a website containing a blog and "live" creator cards with empowering messages for the divine human.)

Lauren Hutton: www.newenergycreator.com/blog (a blog about embodied enlightenment experiences.)

Lindsay Cedolin: www.anewearth.us (a blog supporting the awakening human.)

Norma Delaney: www.compassionatebreath.net (Archives of free webcasts and radio shows that focus on conscious breathing, integration of aspects, and communicating with soul.)

Teal Swan: www.tealswan.com (Free videos on all topics spiritual, with a focus on shadow work.)

The Crimson Circle: www.crimsoncircle.com (The website of a global affiliation of new energy teachers. Free monthly webcast by Adamus Saint-Germain, focusing on embodied enlightenment, plus an abundance of free channelled material.)

Soundtrack for Awakening

Here is a list of my favourite songs related to awakening. I picked the songs based on the lyrics or their vibration. Includes classics and less well-known songs, in various musical styles. You might also want to listen to your favourite love-songs and imagine it's your soul singing to your human self, and human singing to soul.

1. A Fine Frenzy – Pinesong
2. Almir Sater – Tocando em Frente
3. Amirya – Wilderness of the Soul
4. Anders Holte – Timeless Prayer
5. Aurora – Winter Bird
6. Avicii – Wake Me Up
7. Branka Božič – I am
8. Clare Bowen (with Sam Palladino) – Fade into You
9. Claude Debussy – Claire de Lune
10. Damien Rice – Hypnosis, and On Children
11. David Garrett – Viva La Vida
12. Eivør - Falling Free
13. Enya – May It Be
14. Faun - Federkleid
15. Frédéric Chopin – Nocturne op.9
16. Geir Solerod – A Love for Every Day
17. Gerhard Fankhauser – Road to Freedom
18. Imagine Dragons – Radioactive
19. Israel Kamakawiwo'ole – Over the Rainbow
20. James Brown – Super Bad
21. James Taylor – You've Got a Friend
22. Jason Mraz – Living in the Moment
23. Jesse Cook – Fall at your Feet

24. Joshua Kadison – Wild Angel
25. Kay von Randow – Music from the Crystal Caverns
26. Lee Harris & Davor Bozic – Arise
27. Lindsey Stirling - Elements
28. Matt Simons - Catch & Release
29. Metallica – Nothing Else Matters (performed by Lucie Silvas)
30. Mogli - Wanderer
31. Nahko Bear – Aloha Ke Akua
32. Pink Floyd – Breathe
33. Rising Appalachia – Medicine
34. Robert Haig Coxon – The Silent Path
35. Rufus Wainwright – Across the Universe
36. Sarah McLachlan – Angel
37. Selena Gomez – Revival
38. Simon & Garfunkel – The Sound of Silence
39. Supertramp – The Logical Song (performed by Emmerson Nogueira)
40. Taylor Davis – Awakening
41. The Avett Brothers – February Seven
42. Tool - Lateralus
43. Train – Drops of Jupiter
44. Yoham Project – I am that I am

About the Author

Kim Mirjam Seppälä is a Finnish-German consciousness explorer, writer and psychologist in training. She has spent much of her life travelling the world, and also the multidimensional landscapes of consciousness. Her upcoming books will be about *Conscious Romance* and *Creativity as a Path to Consciousness*. She is a facilitator of transformative creative retreats, as well as an actor and playwright for the international *Royal Shaumbra Theater* group. You may contact her via e-mail at: kim.seppala@gmx.com, or read more about her projects on: www.kimseppala.com.

Acknowledgements

With deep gratitude to Shaumbra, the Crimson Circle, Adamus, Kuthumi, Merit, Kuan Yin and other masters who have helped me to remember my true voice. I'd also like to express heartfelt thanks to my friends all around the world, especially Romana for your sovereign sisterhood, and my other friends interviewed in this book for sharing your stories with the world; my human family for providing a safe space for me to be and explore; and my darling Conrado for sharing the adventure of romance and friendship with me. Thank you also Erik for publishing my first book, and Nazar for designing the beautiful cover. And last, but not least, I am grateful for you, dear reader, and the energies you bring into this creation.

www.ingramcontent.com/pod-product-compliance
Lightning Source LLC
Chambersburg PA
CBHW020436130626
46549CB00001B/165